M: Writings '67–'72

WRITINGS '67–'72

BY

JOHN CAGE

WESLEYAN UNIVERSITY PRESS

Middletown, Connecticut

Library of Congress Cataloging in Publication Data

Cage, John.
    M: writings, '67–'72.
    I. Title.
PS3553.A32M2   818'.5'407   72–11051
ISBN 0–8195–4058–7

Manufactured in the United States of America
First edition

To us and all those who hate us,
that the U.S.A. may become just another
part of the world, no more, no less.
(1967, repeated 1973)

CONTENTS

FOREWORD

The title of this book was obtained by subjecting the twenty-six letters of the alphabet to an I Ching chance operation. As I see it, any other letter would have served as well, though M is, to be sure, the first letter of many words and names that have concerned me for many years (music, mushrooms, Marcel Duchamp, M. C. Richards, Morris Graves, Mark Tobey, Merce Cunningham, Marshall McLuhan, my dear friends the Daniels — Minna, for twenty-three years the editor of *Modern Music*, and Mell, early in life and now again in later life, the painter), and recently (mesostics, Mao Tse-tung).

M is also the first letter of *Mureau*, one of the more unconventional texts in this book. *Mureau* departs from conventional syntax. It is a mix of letters, syllables, words, phrases, and sentences. I wrote it by subjecting all the remarks of Henry David Thoreau about music, silence, and sounds he heard that are indexed in the Dover publication of the *Journal* to a series of I Ching chance operations. The personal pronoun was varied according to such operations and the typing was likewise determined. Mureau is the first syllable of the word music followed by the second of the name Thoreau.

Reading the *Journal*, I had been struck by the twentieth-century way Thoreau listened. He listened, it seemed to me, just as composers using technology nowadays listen. He paid attention to each sound, whether it was 'musical' or not, just as they do; and he explored the neighborhood of Concord with the same appetite with which they explore the possibilities provided by electronics. Many of my performances as a musician in recent years have been my vocalizing of *Mureau* or my shouting of another text, scattered like pictures throughout this book, *62 Mesostics re Merce Cunningham*.

My first mesostic was written as prose to celebrate one of Edwin Denby's birthdays. The following ones, each letter of the name being on its own line, were written as poetry. *A given letter capitalized does not occur between it and the preceding capitalized letter.* I thought that I was writing acrostics, but Norman O. Brown pointed out that they could properly be called "mesostics" (row not down the edge but down the middle). Writing about Merce Cunningham for James Klosty's forthcoming book of photographs, I tried to write syntactically as I had in the case of the *Mesostics Re and Not Re Marcel Duchamp*, but the length of Cunningham's name proved to be an obstacle. I suddenly thought that that length together with the name's being down the middle would turn from obstacle to utility if the letters were touching both vertically and horizontally. The poem would then have a spine and resemble Cunningham himself, the dancer. Though this is not the case (these mesostics more resemble waterfalls or ideograms), this is how they came to be made. I used over seven hundred different type faces and sizes available in Letraset and, of course, subjected them to I Ching chance operations. No line has more than one word or syllable. Both syllables and words were obtained from Merce Cunningham's *Changes: Notes on Choreography* and from thirty-two other books most used by Cunningham in relation to his work. The words were subjected to a process which brought about in some cases syllable exchange between two or more of them. This process produced new words not to be found in any dictionary but reminiscent of words everywhere to be found in James Joyce's *Finnegans Wake*.

Rereading *Finnegans Wake* I notice that though Joyce's subjects, verbs, and objects are unconventional, their relationships are the ordinary ones. With the exception of the Ten Thunderclaps and rumblings here and there, *Finnegans Wake* exploys syntax. Syntax gives it a rigidity from which classical Chinese and Japanese were free. A poem by Bashō, for instance, floats in space: any English translation merely takes a snapshot of it; a second translation shows it in quite another light. Only the imagination of the reader limits the number of the poem's possible meanings.

Syntax, according to Norman O. Brown, is the arrangement of the army. As we move away from it, we demilitarize language. This demilitarization of language is conducted in many ways: a single language is pulverized; the boundaries between two or more languages are crossed; elements not strictly linguistic (graphic, musical) are introduced; etc. Translation becomes, if not impossible, unnecessary. Nonsense and silence are produced, familiar to lovers. We begin to actually live together, and the thought of separating doesn't enter our minds.

My work in this field is tardy. It follows the poetry of Jackson MacLow and Clark Coolidge, my analogous work in the field of music, and my first experiments (preceding *Mureau*, but likewise derived from Thoreau's *Journal*), texts for *Song Books* (*Solos for Voice 3–92*), one of which, *Solo for Voice 30*, appears in this book as *Song*. Concrete and sound poets have also worked in this field for many years, though many, it seems to me, have substituted graphic or musical structures for syntactical ones, not having seen that man-made structures themselves (including structures in fields other than language: government in its nonutilitarian aspects, and zoos, for instance) must give way if those beings they were designed to control, whether people, animals, plants, sounds, or words, are to continue on earth to breathe and be.

I now write without syntax and sometimes with it. Thus the *Diary* continues. And the *Mushroom Book* uses both syntax and absence of syntax. The *Diary* now has seven installments, the first three of which appear in *A Year From Monday*.

I hope to finish ten of them. (The year anciently had ten months.) The *Mushroom Book* is an interlude between the sixth and seventh installments of the *Diary*.

I began the *Diary* optimistically in 1965 to celebrate the work of R. Buckminster Fuller, his concern for human needs and world resources, his comprehensive scientific designs for making life on earth an unequivocal success, his insistence that problem solving be continuously regenerative. Fuller predicted that by 1972, following trends, 50% of the world's population would have what they needed for living. The other 50% would rapidly join their ranks. Say by the year 2000. If Fuller's prediction has so far come true, it is not because of anything we Americans have recently done. We have the Chinese to thank, and Mao Tse-tung in particular.

In the fall of 1971 I received a letter from Norman O. Brown. He advised me to stop reading Jacques Ellul (at his advice I had been reading *The Technological Society*) and instead to read *The Chinese Road to Socialism* by E. L. Wheelwright and Bruce McFarlane. "What's happening in China is really important. China maybe has stepped into the future. Perhaps we have to acknowledge that (for our sins) America is no longer the future." My first thought was that Brown, too close to his university students, had received from them an interest in Mao that didn't really belong to him.

When I returned from several bookstores with *The Chinese Road to Socialism* and an anthology of Mao's writings, I expected in reading them to find myself on the other side of the fence.

I knew it would be necessary to concentrate my attention on world improvement, to eliminate from my mind all thoughts about art. Contemporary Chinese arts are timely advertisements for the revolution, not significant expressions of it. Fortunately I had listened when Jasper Johns said, "I can imagine a society without any art at all, and it is not a bad society."

I was deeply touched in the Wheelwright and McFarlane book by the account of the material and spiritual changes in Chinese environment, technology, and society. I was immediately glad that seven hundred million people were no longer divided between what Fuller calls the haves and the have-nots. I was cheered by the news that one-fifth of the world's population were "fighting self-interest" and "serving the people." Just the news that people of all ages (the very young and the very old, and the usual 'able-bodied') were working together to turn desert into garden was refreshing: I had become numb from the social habit (practiced indiscriminately in the U.S.A., only politically in China) of getting rid of people, even killing them when feasible. I can't forget visits to my mother who lived the last years of her life unwillingly in a "comfortable" New Jersey nursing home. She begged to be taken home but her home no longer existed.

Wheelwright's and McFarlane's observations of changes in Chinese human nature were recently corroborated for me by Jumay Chu, a young American dancer who returned in the fall of '72 from a visit to China. Jumay told me she had asked a Chinese factory worker whether he was happy. (He was doing work to which he had been assigned that she herself wouldn't have enjoyed doing because it was repetitive and boring.) The factory worker didn't understand her question. He was doing his work as part of China's work; he was one person in the Chinese family.

In Mao's writings I skipped over the texts which are those of a general speaking to his soldiers, though I read carefully the rules he gave them regarding right conduct among persons of occupied land: to assist them with their work, to care for their well-being and property. "We Communists are like seeds and the people are like the soil. Wherever we go, we must unite with the people, take root and blossom among them." Though the history of the Chinese Revolution is a history of violence, it includes the Long March, a grand retreat that reminds me of the Thoreau-influenced social actions of Gandhi, Martin Luther King, and the Danes in their response to Hitler's invasion.

I felt very close to Mao when I read in his biography that as a young man he had studied with great interest the texts of anarchism. And his admonitions to the people during the Chinese Cultural Revolution, including the very young, admonitions to revolt against authority, including his own authority, were ones with which I wholeheartedly concur. "It is right to rebel." "Bombard the headquarters." Observed from a Western distance, Mao often seemed to be leading China into chaos. But it was to Chaos himself, in Kwang-tse's writings, that the Spirit of the Clouds put his questions when he felt the need to improve the world.

Throughout his thinking, I admired Mao's clear-headedness. He saw, for instance, that the solution of the Chinese problem was necessarily specifically Chinese. It would be wrong for it to be merely Russian. The largest number of Chinese people were peasants and the largest number of peasants were poor. The revolution in China was therefore to begin with them and in relation to their needs.

This looking to the masses made me think of Fuller, his vision of a world society in which all people, no matter their age, are properly students. The good life is a university, different from those we now have, from which while living we never graduate. The World Revolution to come ("the greatest of them all"), apolitical, nonviolent, intelligent because comprehensively and regeneratively problem solving (cf. Mao: We must learn to look at problems all-sidedly, seeing the reverse as well as the obverse side of things) is a "Student Revolution."

I began then to search for the common denominator between Mao and Fuller, and, when I came across seemingly irreconcilable differences between the two, I decided to listen to both. For instance, Fuller's advice, "Don't change man; change environment" and Mao's directive: "Remould people to their very souls; revolutionize their thinking."

Daisetz Suzuki often pointed out that Zen's nondualism arose in China as a result of problems encountered in translating India's Buddhist texts. Pali had syntax; Chinese did not. Indian words for concepts in opposition to one another did not exist in Chinese. *Fixity* became *mountain-mountain; flexibility* became *springweather-springweather*. Buddhism became Zen Buddhism. Looking for an Indian precedent, Chinese patriarchs chose the Flower Sermon of the Buddha, a sermon in which no word was spoken. Reading Mao's text *On Contradiction*, I think of it as twentieth-century expression of nondualistic thought.

While I was writing the texts in this book, I was also writing music: *HPSCHD* (with Lejaren Hiller), *Cheap Imitation* (first for piano solo and now also for orchestra, twenty-four to ninety-six musicians, without conductor), *Song Books*. And I initiated a number of performances which have not involved notation: *Musicircus* (bringing together under one roof as much of the music of the surrounding community as one practicably can), *Reunion* (with David Tudor, Lowell Cross, David Behrman, Gordon Mumma, Marcel and Teeny Duchamp), *33 1/3* (a music utility operated by the audience), *Demonstration of the Sounds of the Environment* (three hundred people silently following an I Ching determined path through Milwaukee's University of Wisconsin campus), and *Mureau* not vocalized by myself alone but together with others (Western Michigan University, Kalamazoo).

In 1952, with Morton Feldman, Christian Wolff, Earle Brown, and David Tudor, I had taken steps to make a music that was just sounds, sounds free of judgments about whether they were 'musical' or not, sounds free of memory and taste (likes and dislikes), sounds free of fixed relations between two or more of them (musical syntax, or glue, as Henry Cowell called it when he introduced one of our concerts in the 'fifties at the New School).

Since the theory of conventional music is a set of laws exclusively concerned with 'musical' sounds, having nothing to say about noises, it had been clear from the beginning that what was needed was a music based on noise, on noise's lawlessness. Having made such an anarchic music, we were able later to include in its performance even so-called musical sounds.

The next steps were social, and they are still being taken. We need first of all a music in which not only are sounds just sounds but in which people are just people, not subject, that is, to laws established by any one of them even if he is "the composer" or "the conductor." Finally (as far as I can see at present), we need a music which no longer prompts talk of audience participation, for in it the division between performers and audience no longer exists: a music made by everyone.

I learned this in Kalamazoo. In a room seating two hundred volunteers having untrained voices, we rehearsed *Mureau*, not attempting to make words clear, but paying attention to individual letters. The feelings we had and the sounds we heard were such that we all looked forward to the next evening's performance. This was given in a different place, a hall seating three thousand. When it began, something like the sound of the rehearsal was to be heard, though it was not so impressive. The social situation soon changed. Not all, but some, in one way or another, aggressively drew attention to themselves. It was possible to enjoy what happened (many of the audience themselves became performers). But the old splits remained: between performers and audience, between proscenium stage and seats in rows facing towards it. No improvement in society was exemplified; the music we could use had been made the day before. What's required is a music that requires no rehearsal.

This is my deepest conviction. However, I've been obliged in the case of the orchestral version of *Cheap Imitation* to include in the directions a *Minimum Rehearsal Requirement*.

The first performance of *Cheap Imitation* (with the essential twenty-four of the ninety-six parts) was announced for early May (1972) by Gaudeamus, the Dutch musical organization. The conductor (who does not perform in the concert but acts as a coach during rehearsals) was Jan Stulen and the musicians were especially chosen by the Mobile Ensemble. When I arrived in The Hague the day of the performance, I found that the musicians were working on the music for the first time. It proved too difficult for presentation following a single rehearsal. At that evening's concert we therefore presented a rehearsal of the first movement. The next day at another concert when the work was to have been repeated, we managed, quite well, to get through two movements and also without conductor. This obliged the musicians to listen to one another, a thing they rarely do. Gaudeamus, embarrassed, arranged to have the work played on the Holland Festival a month or so later; they assured me that it would be well prepared. However, when I arrived in Holland for the final rehearsal, I discovered that not only was the orchestra's final rehearsal their first but that many of the musicians had not bothered to look at the music and that Jan Stulen had been replaced by a former pupil of Boulez who himself said as the rehearsal began, "I think this work has three movements; is that true?" After hearing a few miserable attempts to play the first phrases, I spoke to the musicians about the deplorable state of society (not only of musical society), and I withdrew the piece from the evening's program. By having written *Cheap Imitation*, I've provided, I think, a means for opening the ears of orchestral musicians and enabling them to make music instead of, as now, only money to pay their bills. I am convinced that they play other music just as badly as they play mine. However, in the case of *Cheap Imitation*, there are no climaxes, no harmonies, no counterpoints in which to hide one's lack of devotion. This lack of devotion is not to be blamed on particular individuals (whether they are musicians who don't listen or vacationists who leave garbage beside waterfalls); it is to be blamed on the present organization of society; it is the raison d'être for revolution.

What can I as a composer do to bring about the revolution? Shall I give up working with trained musicians and go on from what I learned at Kalamazoo? Or shall I continue my efforts to make the symphony orchestra an instance of an improved society, and forget about those two hundred people in Michigan who don't know how to sing anyway? I can do both. I can work in the society as it intolerably structured is, and I can also work in it as hopefully unstructured it will in the future be.

I have the example of Marcel Duchamp. A paper bag, a cigar, my membership card in Czechoslovakia's mushroom society, anything became a work of art simply because Duchamp was willing to sign it. At the same time he spent the last twenty years of his life making the most rigorously controlled work of art that anyone has ever made: by means of a Spanish brick wall and a locked wooden door with two peepholes in it, he controlled the distance from which *Étant Donnés* was to be observed. The extraordinary contradiction between this work and the world around us — to which Duchamp's willingness to sign anything was the best of all possible introductions — is the contradiction in which we have the room to live.

> Not less than two weeks before a projected performance each musician shall be given his part. During the first week he will learn the melody, at least those phrases of it in which he participates. He is to learn, among other matters, to play double sharps and double flats without writing in simpler "equivalent" notes.
>
> During the second week there will be an orchestral rehearsal on each day, each rehearsal lasting one and one-half hours. If, at any time, it appears that any member of the orchestra does not know his part, he is to be dismissed...

(Cf. Mao Tse-tung: "What should our policy be towards non-Marxist ideas? As far as unmistakable counter-revolutionaries and saboteurs of the socialist cause are concerned, the matter is easy: we simply deprive them of their freedom of speech.")

> ...If as a result one of the essential twenty-four parts is missing, the projected performance is to be cancelled.

I am, of course, on my last legs, so that, as I put my foot down, it is doubtful whether it will have any effect. If the structure of the symphony orchestra remains as it is, even conscientious musicians will not be able to follow my rule. They are merely employees who must do what the conductor tells them to. The conductor must do his work in such a way that its costs do not exceed the budget approved by the board of trustees. My rehearsal schedule is expensive. There isn't enough time. The Dutch musicians each month give more concerts than there are days; each concert has several pieces (all of them need running through). "To play your music," one of them told me, "you have to change your mind with regard to music itself. How can you expect ninety-six people to do that?"

But it's not just ninety-six people who must change their minds. We are now closer to four than to three billion. Not so long ago the world was called a global village. Buckminster Fuller calls it spaceship earth. Every one of us is on it.

The party's nearly over. But the guests are going to stay: they have no place else to go. People who weren't invited are beginning to arrive. The house is a mess. We must all get together and without saying a word clean it up.

M: Writings ʼ67–ʼ72

DIARY: HOW TO IMPROVE THE WORLD (YOU WILL ONLY MAKE MATTERS WORSE) CONTINUED 1968 (REVISED)

XCI. Laughter. **Computer music.** **No
one mentions secrecy.** **Machine
language.** **Accumulation of
sub-routines, sub-routines anyone may
use.** *Truth's not true.* *We were
speaking of individuality (Thoreau's
"respect for the individual"): Brown
connected 'atom' with 'individual'
(they've both been split).* *An
individual, having no separate soul, is a
time-span, a collection of changes.* *Our
nature's that of Nature.* *Nothing's
fixed.* *Excepting everything, there's
nothing to respect.* *He'd go along,
Brown said, with "the here and the
now."* Why, in recent wars, does
U.S. favor the south against the
north? Non-strategic. Fight *against*
the south: South, say, Africa, siding with
African nations to the north. Whites
giving their lives for blacks!
Soldiers would return victorious, pockets
full of diamonds. XCII. June 23.
(1840) "We Yankees are not so far from
right,"—(Thoreau)—"who answer one
question by asking another. Yes and
No are lies. A true answer will not aim
to establish anything, but rather to set
all well afloat." *Mentioning opposites, he
called them correlatives.* *Fuller
calls them complements.* *Taking down the*

4

*fences.   Frontiers describe what's
beyond as well as what's enclosed.*

Three.   **I noticed the nurses were kind to
her.   "Naturally they are.   If you
like people, they like you."**   When I
received the letter that said I'd be
required to sign a form stating I
didn't want to overthrow the
government (otherwise I wouldn't get
the position I'd been offered), I asked
my friends what to do.   They said: Sign
the form; take the job; go on with your
work.   *XCIII.   The Israeli-Arab
situation's hopeless.   Jewish friends
I talked to didn't make good sense.
Quote: After ages suffering, aren't
you glad we finally have a little
success?   Unquote.   Suggesting Jews
use technological know-how to benefit
Arabs, I was given this reply: Israelis
wanted to, Arabs wouldn't let'em.*
Weather changed.   It's freezing.   In
no time at all the temperature
dropped a total of forty degrees.
Uglification.   We're good at it.
Single individuals without
encountering obstacles darken the corners
where they are.   When Gandhi was asked what
he thought of Western Civilization, he
said, "It would be nice."   **One thing we
refuse is to employ an answering
service.   It's of the greatest urgency—a
matter of ethics even—that we be able to
reach one another.   Those who are
selfish will change their minds re
interruptions (i.e. become
superficially ethical): incoming telephone**

calls will be the means by which one's
social credit exceeds a basic economic
security (social usefulness
measured).   XCIV.   When I entered the
house, I noticed some very
interesting music was being played.
After a drink or two, I asked my
hostess what it was. She said, ''You
can't be serious?''   *Scientists are*
sometimes not scientific.   Take
atomic garbage.   First they put it in
rivers and streams.   Then someone
noticed the waters began to boil.   Now just
as cats do after shitting, scientists
dig a trench, put the garbage in it,
cover it up, and then forget about it.
Ecological thinking.   "Decisions to
make."   *There must be times for him, as*
there are for me, when, looking in my
direction expecting to say hello, I
pass by preoccupied.   Artificial death
(something we invented).   XCV.   Coal and
oil we use are being replenished.
Fossilization.   It takes ages.
Buckminster Fuller, speaking in financial
terms, describes underground energy
sources as capital sources to
differentiate them from those above
ground which he describes as income.
Fuller advises saving capital for
emergencies.   *Changed, mind includes*
even itself.   Unchanged, nothing gets in or
out.   I was grounded.   The pilot
refused to fly.   I took to the woods.
Found *Tricholoma equestre* (first time
I ever did).   Then in Ohio, on the way to

another airport, found *Pleuroti,*
Collybiae.   *Revolution.*   **Two people**
making same kind of music is one
music too many.   XCVI.   Unripe fruit.
Asked Fuller about atomic energy.   *He*
didn't smile.   *His comment: It's partly*
income, partly capital.   **I was given a**
book of photographs and poems.   The
photographs're nineteen inches wide,
only a few inches high.   They are shots
of the Midwest.   Going to Illinois, I
took this book along as aesthetic
insurance against the land and air
I'd be living in.   In the course of telling
what she'd seen while traveling around
the world, Mrs. Cunningham mentioned the
camels in Japan.   Mr. Cunningham said,
"You must mean the camels in Egypt."
Going on, Mrs. Cunningham said
parenthetically, "Of course that's what I
mean."   *XCVII.*   *Music (not*
composition).   The U.S. government
has joined the protest movement.
Postage stamp bears the motto: Search
for Peace.   Another commemorates
Thoreau.   (Wanderers.   No notion of where
we'll be going next.)   Driving to
Chicago, no need for art.   Land's an
ocean.   Earth's black.   Trees, even
those with leaves, visible.   Pheasants,
frightened, run the road from China.
Spring sponges.   Fall stumpies and
quirines.   Pinkies.   He got his hands dirty
so we could live.   (We, too, are
trees.)   That I'm grateful costs him no
time.   Coming back from the pilgrimage,
they tell us the roof is leaking.   It's

good our heads're worn-out.   (His
ideas are getting in.)   He's as serious and
frivolous as Chaos.   "When?" was the
question she asked.   Then added: "Each
second counts."   XCVIII.   "Why'd you
hit him in the first place?"   "I
didn't.   I only hit him when he hit me
back."   Moon.   Tides.   Asked why the
radios didn't work, she said, "We bought
the big one for seventy-five dollars
and it didn't work.   Then we bought the
little one.   It doesn't work either, but
it only cost ten dollars."
"Classification . . . ceases when it's no
longer possible to establish
oppositions."   (Government's
outmoded.)   To improve society, spend
more time with people whom you haven't
met.   Paul Goodman: "A man . . . draws now,
as far as he can, on the natural force
in him that is no different from what it
will be in the new society . . . Merely
continuing to exist and act in nature
and freedom, a free man wins the victory,
establishes the new society. . . ."
(Drawing the Line).   XCIX.   We do what no
one else does.   Economy.   (We do not
believe in "human nature.")   We are
nouveau-riches.   Beyond that, we are
criminals.   There, outside the law, we
tell the truth.   For this reason, we
exploit technology.   Circumstances
determine our actions.   *Wind.*   *Straw*
that will break Christmas's back: we'll
already have what someone intends to give
us.   *Friendship.*   The price-system
and government that enforces it are on

the way out.   They're going out the way a
fire does.   Protest actions fan the
flames of a dying fire.   Protest helps to
keep the government going.   *Energy*
from outer space.   Radioaction in a form
not requiring fission/fusion.   C.   She
bought a number of towels to give as
Christmas presents to people in the
community.   By mistake she gave them all
to me.   **Violence.**   If revolution's
colored, include white.   White and
black look well together.   **Gentle**
Thursday.   My plan was to do my work and
then join Cincinnati's Be-In.   At 4:30 Andy
telephoned to say it had petered
out.   *Predictions of astrologers.   "The*
start of a deep transformation on
earth."   We're leaving the Piscean
age, entering the Aquarian one.   We'll be
living in a situation of overlap,
interplay, global unity, universal
understanding, collective peace and
harmony.   **Subjectivity.**   *Kill two birds*
with one stone.   Stop using oil and
coal.   We'll keep them there in the
earth against a rainy day.   Large cause
of air-pollution'll be eliminated.   We'll
use energies above ground—sun,
wind, tides.   Air'll automatically become
what it was: something good to breathe.
CI.   Sri Ramakrishna not only lived as a
man, a woman, a monkey: he lived for
six months as a plant, standing on one
leg in ecstasy.   We are not arranging
things in order (that's the function of
the utilities): we are merely

facilitating processes so that anything can
happen.   After leaving Tokyo's
airport, Itu Hisuki wrote this
letter: "Mr. Baggage Man American
Airlines United States of Los Angeles
Gentleman dear sir: I damn seldom where
my suitcase are.   She no fly.   You no
more fit to baggage master than for
crysake that's all I hope.   What's the
matter you?   Itu Hisuki"   *CII.*   *We*
think at the same time others (animates,
inanimates) think.   We are intimate in
advance with whatever will happen.
Not blood.   Just relationship.   **Power**
and profit structures're out of cahoots
with current technology.   Aware of new
inventions, corporations put them
aside, waiting for competitive reasons
until they're obliged to use new
gimmicks.   Possessed of the atom bomb,
they are hog-tied.   They dare not
use it.   Alice.   Wonderland.   Robert
Duncan told me his poetry was picked up
from other people.   The only time he
felt, he said, like using quotation
marks was when the words he wrote
were his.   Say the country's based on
law and order as after each riot
politicians maintain.   Instead of
allocating funds for summer
entertainments in Roman efforts to
distract the masses, it would be more
effective to prohibit advertising (TV
commercials in particular) so that the poor
wouldn't know what it was they were
missing.   *CIII.*   *She'd been born in*

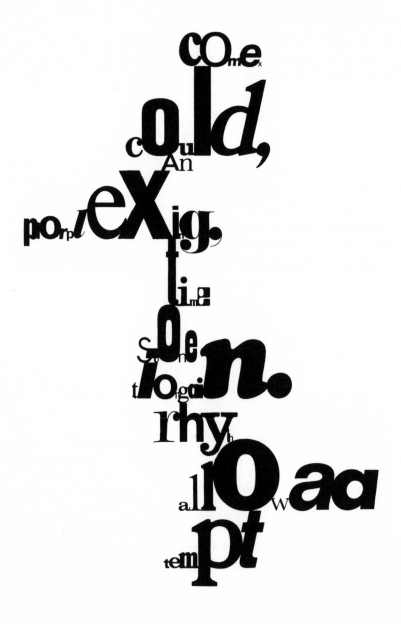

her summer home overlooking a mountain
lake formerly owned by her family, now
shared with Boy Scouts.   Carpenter
whom she'd employed, whom she'd known
since childhood, always treated her
like an outsider.   While he rested, she
asked, "What's the difference
between natives and outsiders?"
"Natives," he replied, "eat indoors
and shit outdoors, outsiders eat
outdoors and shit indoors."   **Our flights**
are interrupted by overnight stays in
airport motels.   No one knows where we
are.   McLuhan said it.   We're like
the Middle Ages.   People building
cathedrals.   Glorification.   No need
for God: just Universe.   Doing
something we don't know how to do.   No
technique.   Dad used to say: If someone
says, "Can't," that indicates the thing for
you to do.   **CIV.   Spent several hours**
searching through a book trying to
find the idea I'd gotten out of it.   I
couldn't find it.   I still have the idea.
        X.   He said he'd never heard my music.
        "You haven't missed a thing."   Letter
                to Tenney: It's useless to play
        lullabies for those who cannot go to
sleep.   Retaliating, they'll put you in
        prison.   We'll have lost synergetic
advantage working with you gave us.
        (How many are we?   You also
        benefited.)   You're right, of course
(they're wrong).   But you don't intend,
        do you, to perpetuate such
distinctions?   First thing he did after
taking the job as school principal was to
sign his resignation, explaining he didn't

want people to feel obliged to keep him
around.   Then he fired the librarian,
permitting students free access to
books.   Instead of being stolen or not
returned, inventory after one year
showed there were fifty more books
than there had been originally.   CV.
"Common sense."   **We do what we do by means
of contradiction.**   *Gravity's a local
event, one of many in the electrostatic
field.   Find means whereby one can tune
in or out of the gravitational field
of this or that body in space.
(Nonviolent space travel.)   Find
other uses of gravity for those
who're living on Earth.*   Consider
incestuous any marriage between two people
of the same race, country, or faith.
**No idea how it happens.   Even if we had
an idea (which's been shown to
facilitate its escaping our notice)
it'd still happen.**   Met John Platt.
He suggests that contraceptive substances
be added to basic foods: flour, rice,
sugar, salt, etc.   The human species
would become normally unreproductive.
Should a couple wish to have a child,
they'd go to special stores to procure
their food.   Every child a wanted child.
CVI.   hard clay the earth/ iron-weed the
corn/ that was my crib   (Teeny fifteen
years old)   *If the situation is hopeless,
we have nothing to worry about.*
Post-graduate studies.   *Quantum Theory.*
January.   Drove across Ding Darling
Sanctuary on Sanibel off Florida's
western coast.   Saw vulture; hawks;

ducks and smaller birds; white, blue,

   black and grey taller birds, poised on
branches or stalking the shallow waters.
Man got out of his car behind us to
photograph.   We asked him what kind of
      bird it was.   He said, "That's a grey
      heron, five feet tall."   **During the**
      discussion, she asked a question
about education.   Answer: People together
      without restrictions in a situation
abundantly implemented.   She asked another.
   "People to whom it never occurs to ask:
         Mother!   What shall I do now?"   She
   turned and left the room.   CVII.   Hands
aren't possessive.   They belong to the
same body.   *They taught us art was*
   self-expression.   You had to have
      "something to say."   They were wrong:
you don't have to say anything.   Think of
   the others as artists.   Art's
      self-alteration.   ("Charlotte
Thrasher came to me late last evening
   to say that she'd jumped a wave,
   taken the way of the fishes and would
      not return until morning.")   If we
start with the past and move to the
present, we go from pleasure to
irritation.   Do you know what's happening?
      The Indian mind is moving.   It'll
handle computers, cybernetics,
   what-have-you, better than other
minds can.   **CVIII.   Global Civil War.**
Family as it now stands doesn't work.
   North, south, brothers are quarreling,
      running to one parent or the other
      to obtain a favorable judgment.   **A**
mother telephoned to ask whether her son

was coming home for Christmas. **"No," he**
replied, "I love you, but I'm going west.
You and Dad're always bickering." Examine
thoughts and words, written or
spoken, weeding out those that are
dead. Dead ones are those concerning
aggression. Konrad Lorenz: the evolution
of human nature. Toshi Ichiyanagi says:
Funny thing about that Itu Hisuki story
is that Itu Hisuki is not a very
Japanese name. CIX. Reading
Thoreau's *Journal*, I discover any idea
I've ever had worth it's salt. (Oppressive
laws were made to keep two Irishmen from
fighting in the streets.) The door
opened. He walked in, turned on the light,
sat down, died. The light is still on.
No one turned it off. **India: a luxury we**
can no longer afford. **Graves said:**
Imagine that you're dreaming. **I told**
Ellen to stretch her visit to the
limit, then stay another day.
Government's contemporary if its
activities aren't interrupted by the
action of technology. *Americans, to*
remain rich, strong, required to
curtail world travel, stop investment in
foreign industries. *Ergo:*
Washington's behind the times. CX. At
the present moment, the question is: Do
I have enough change for another beer?
More important question: Is there
enough food and drink for everyone who is
living? Civilization is Hamletized
(people are dying right and left): To
be or not to be. That is the question.
Tempo no longer exists. **Just**

quantity.　　Say there are only a few sounds.
Say they're loud.　　What to do?　　Jump?　　"But
still Vietnam goes on!　　And what of the
concentration camps in California,
etc? . . . Who shall be called to serve
'their country' in them . . . ?
Malcolm"　　Criticism's not the time to
think.　　Think ahead of time.　　Buckminster
Fuller.　　CXI.　　Tenney wrote to say: "What's
required . . . is . . . radical eclecticism
(Ives) . . . 'every composer's duty.' . . .
More power to Fuller . . . to
revolutionary guerrillas . . . to Christian
pacifists . . . to flower children . . . to
hippies . . . acidheads . . . beatniks, diggers
and provos . . . to the militant blacks . . . to
those who keep asking questions."　　We
were at opposite ends of the hall.　　We
left our separate rooms and are now in
the hall itself.　　Problems of
governments are not inclusive enough.　　We
need (we've got them) global problems in
order to find global solutions.
Problems connected with sounds were
insufficient to change the nature of
music.　　We had to conceive of silence in
order to open our ears.　　We need to
conceive of anarchy to be able
whole-heartedly to do whatever another
tells us to.　　CXII.　　It's been dangerous.
Still is.　　Warnings are constantly
given.　　Furthermore, though we gave
our lives, our actions seemed superficial.
That is, we went out rather than in.
Premise was: opposites are intimately
connected.　　Were we to start again,

we'd start from a consideration
(constellation of ideas).   **What we
have would be no uglier called by
another name.   Veblen called it the
price-system.   Mills called it the Power
Elite.   It's probably no more than
ninety-nine people who don't know what
they're doing.   They're involved in
high finance.   Fascinating form of
gambling.**   We sent music outdoors as
one sends children to play, so
grown-ups could get what they were
doing done.   CXIII.   McHale: "The . . .
interdependence of all nations . . . to
maintain . . . daily operation (of airlines,
telecommunications and other . . . global
services), now renders ineffective . . .
attempts at unilateral action based on
imaginary sovereign autonomy.   We
are . . . hypnotized by such notions . . .
though they are no longer operable
in the real world.   When we went by
mail-boat to visit Fuller, the fog was so
thick you couldn't see where you were
going.   That night he talked by
candlelight.   In the morning the fog had
lifted.   All the islands of the Penobscot
were visible, even the ones in the
distance.   It was like Matsushima, but
larger.   We'll keep the Stop and Go signs—
even their colors: red and green.
But we'll give the signs the ability
to observe traffic so that the Go sign
will not appear when there are no cars
waiting to go.   *CXIV.   Sleep's what
we need.   It produces an emptiness in*

us into which sooner or later energies

flow.   *Metabolism.*   Combine nursing homes

with nursery schools.   Bring very old

and very young together: they interest

one another.   Farting, don't think,

just fart.   Sign above the toilet:

Have patience!   The toilet *will*

flush.   Just give it time to fill up.

Artilleryman, flying home, anxious to

return to Vietnam, said there's a job

to be done.   If soldiers were free

to kill anyone anytime anywhere, war,

he said, could be won.   Army rules

cramp our style.   E.g., rubber trees

aren't to be damaged in any way.

CXV.   Books one picked up and put down

over a period, say, of ten years,

picking them up on the eleventh to

discover the impossibility of putting

them down.   What's the arithmetic of

this?   The heavenly city's no longer

walled-in: it has gone up in space.

Talking about education, Fuller said

he preferred talking to people whose

minds weren't, say, more than

half-filled up.   Furthermore, a child,

he said, by the mere fact of being born

is educated.   We're no longer willing

to be entertained piecemeal—recitals of

this and that, megalopolitan museums here

and there.   We insist on continuous

use of aesthetic faculty.   *CXVI.*

Computers're bringing about a situation

that's like the invention of harmony.

Sub-routines are like chords.   No one

would think of keeping a chord to himself.

You'd give't to anybody who wanted it.

You'd welcome alterations of it.
Sub-routines are altered by a single punch.
We're getting music made by man himself:
not just one man. **STZ.** **Some**
programming errors arise from successive
operations without recourse between to
zero (an error that wasn't recognized
as such in 12-tone music). **Neti-Neti:**
the "nothing-in-between."
Society'll work without fatal error if
(Thoreau) it's governed not at all.
Store zero. Planes that are used in
Vietnam are planes left over from a
previous war. A new bomber just in order
to get up in the air gets to a point
beyond its destination. You'd think that
our leadership would manage to keep
abreast of technological advance, and
choose adversaries who are
positioned at the proper distance. **CXVII.**
World body. We learn nothing from the
things we know. The taxi-driver
insisted people have to have other people
to hate. I remained silent. Before
I left the cab, he changed his tune.
Comprehensive design. Meister
Eckhart spoke of the soul's simplicity.
But Nature's complicated. We must get
rid of the soul or train it to deal
with countless numbers of things.
Likewise the ego, its dreams, its value
judgments. (We just might make it.)
Dharma is being revitalized by sense
perceptions and extensions of them.
Giving up true and false. The mind, like
a computer, produces a print-out.
It's on the palms of our hands. CXVIII.

Why keep connecting him with "his"
work?   Don't you see that he's a human
being, whereas his work isn't?   If, for
instance, you decided to kick his work and
him, you would, wouldn't you, have to
perform two actions rather than a
single one?   The more he leaves his
work, the more usable it becomes (room
in it for others).   Study universe.
Arrange matters so things are where they
belong.   Radioactive refuse?   Belongs
out in space.   Past a certain threshold,
it'll go of its own accord to the Sun.
He said something.   I understood
something.   Communication?   **Edwin
Schlossberg and Jon Dieges conducted
a class in Design at the University
of Southern Illinois (Design in
Buckminster Fuller's sense).   Students did
research and wrote papers,
but gave them to one another instead of
handing them in to the teachers.   At
the last session, one of the
students came up to Eddie and asked him
what his last name was.**

36 MESOSTICS RE AND NOT RE DUCHAMP

For Shigeko Kubota

a utility aMong
swAllows
is theiR
musiC.
thEy produce it mid-air
to avoid coLliding.

there is no Difference between life and death.
(sUzuki.)
it is Consistent
to say deatH is the most
importAnt thing one day and the next day
to say life is the Most
imPortant thing.

getting olD?
then give Up. or
Continue.
go Home.
chAnge
your Mind.
still comPosing?

aDvanced
stUdy:
suitCases.
Home'll
be Africa.
crêMe fraiche followed by
3 kinds of Potatoes.

just before Midnight
wAiting
in the stReet
(Costa brava):
for all thE
worLd a handsome young man.

Don't
yoU ever want to win?
(impatienCe.)
How do you
mAnage to live with
just one sense of huMor?
she must have Persuaded him to smile.

the wind-break becaMe
A
woRk of art
(it began Casually
likE
the firepLace).

avoid woMen
And gold,
sRi ramakrishna advised.
"but that is not the way to Cross
thE stream.
foLlow me."

Me?
i sleep eAsily
undeR
any aCoustic condition.
as hE said:
Lullaby.

intention Disappears
with Use.   (johns.)
aspeCts
otHer
thAn
those we had in Mind
Produce attention.

the Disease
is not Under
Control.
taking tHe doctor's suggestion
thAt i have
My hair cut
Proved useless.

why did she invite Me to lunch?
A
cuRious
oCcasion
including a princEss who was seated
at the other tabLe.

he said, i do not believe that i aM.
he wAs, as he also said,
a bReather.
he Could
brEathe
effortLessly.

we reMember
thAt
he had stopped woRking,
even though we're now Conscious
hE
never reLaxed for a moment.

reMove god
from the world of ideAs.
Remove government,
politiCs from
sociEty. keep sex, humor,
utiLities. Let private property go.

they told Me
someone who hAd a
pRoblem
engaged him in a disCussion of it.
hE gave no advice
but the other Left relieved.

the sounDs
of the bUgle
were out of my Control,
tHough without
my hAving
Made the effort
they wouldn't have been Produced.

are they relateD
or Unrelated
to the arthritiC condition?
a gatHering of differences
or An
accuMulation, more of the same?
(the new Pains.)

More
And
moRe
rules are esCaping our
noticE. they were
secretLy put in the museum.

but who will Do all the work
(the décor for *walkaroUnd time*)?
and to prepare the leCture
He
hAd agreed to prepare proved less
interesting than to change his Mind about doing so.
on the other hand, it amused him to Perform as a professional musician.

inviteD
oUt
he'd Cut
the evening sHort.
At
hoMe
he'd suggest we stay uP later.

the olD
sUit,
the blaCk one
i tHrew out,
wAs found,
Mended,
and Put back in the closet.

we renteD
an aUtomobile,
and drove aCross italy
from one Hill-town
to Another,
200 Miles
to sPoleto.

say we have one probleM
              And
     one hundRed
solutions. instead of Choosing
         just onE of them, we
use them aLl.

     n. o. brown: atoM
            smAshed
makes thundeR.
      radiCal
     changE
is therefore simpLe.

                  since other Men
                     mAke
                     aRt,
                  he Cannot.
                    timE
                  is vaLuable.

        to Modify
         Animal
behaviouR
         Count
     up to tEn
     before Laughing.

              you Must
                hAng
            youR paintings on the walls.
               "i Can't stand to look
          at thEm."
that's why you must hang them on the waLls.

finally he telephoneD.
it had been hard to Understand
what had Caused
Him
not to Appear.
he said there were Many things
we should have the oPportunity to discuss.

the church has an iMpressive
fAcade,
but a Rundown interior.
glanCing at it quickly,
i lEft. now i have to go back.
the paintings in a side chapeL, they say, are well worth seeing.

cross the briDge.
that's where he foUnd
the stiCks
on wHich
the illuminAted
feMale
was Placed.

when we Decided to go to the falls,
he said he woUldn't go with us.
in Cadaquès too
He
Always stayed
at hoMe
when we went to swim and Play chess on the beach.

the iMpossibility of
repeAted actions;
the loss of memoRy:
to reaCh
thEse
two's a goaL.

More
thAn
nouRishment,
eating's a soCial occasion.
hE ate
very Little.

questions i Might
hAve
leaRned
to ask Can
no longEr
receive repLies.

the telegraM
cAme.
i Read it.
death we expeCt,
but all wE get
is Life.

MUREAU

sparrowsitA gROsbeak betrays *itself* by that peculiar squeakariEFFECT
OF SLIGHTEst tinkling measures soundness ingpleasa We hear! Does
it not rather hear us? sWhen he hears the telegraph, he thinksthose
bugs have issued forthThe owl touches the stops, wakes reverb
erations *d gwalky* In verse there is no inherent mus*ic eof*sttakestak
es a man to make a room silent It takes to make a roomIt IS A Young a
ppetite and the appETITEFOR IsHe Oeyssee morningYou hear scream o
f great hawka yd*gh bo*dyShelie being*s*ilencelt would be noblest to sing
with the windTo hear a neighbor *singing!* u it wood The triosteum a
day or twob mtryTheysays to-we*e, to-wee*calling to his team lives he
ard over high *open fields*day instead of the drum thensav pa with youn
g birdswith young birdsfrom a truck ndat every postt ed der oglects
in the meantime o pi at so *piercing ders ache*Theyo ato sing in earnest
seven now chU ASISu gddd gheasu s iot ei gh c n ch siYou woul
d thiNK MUSIC *was being b*orn again off *Toad*s are still heard at *eve*
*ning*cRIckets'Echo is an indepen*dent sound Rhyme and* tell his story and
breathe himselfbreathe A shrill loud alarm is *incessantly repeated* t
heheroic hovers from *over the* pond *the clear* metallic *scream* they
*went off wi*th a shriller craikThey go off with a hoARSer chuck ch
uck noair hear sharp, screaming notes rending the airThis suggests *wha*
t perpetual fl*ow of spirit woul*d produceA thrumming beyond and thr
oughimportant Every *one can* CAll to mind instances mill Trees creak
*ringingWe could not hear the b*irdsIs *the third* note confined to this
season? Little frogs begin to peep toward sundown noonhorn is heard e
choing from sh*ore to shore*of perchwith a loud, *ripp*ling rustle t
hink larmedand makes life seem serene a*nd grandinex*pressibly serene
and gr*and apparently* afrai*dwith more vigor and promise bells*lee u*t*tering
that sign-like note verwarm and *moist not much of* the toad ev so ch
eaply e*nriched for the listening*of that word "sound" and *am the scene*
of liferingter viMusicand mel in melody ein the next townand fire
openest all her senses *n k swhich they* do not rememberee eeac*h recess o*
F THE WOODA Ea what various distinct sounds ve *heard there* deep in
*the woodsh*n AND echo along the shore ymORE THAN A Rodnd a sa stead
y, BReathing, cricket-like soundhunse*e*n and unheard *May it be such*
summ*er as it suggests into* the woodsThere is in*wardness even in* the
mosqu*itoes' hum*T*r*ees hav*e* been so many empty music-*halls* heard from th
e depth of the woodnig*H*T The toward nighttheir hour has s*erenity who a*
m*h*umming past so busily lungs sweet *flowingfro*m farther or nearerhuRR
IED RIPPLING NOtes in the yardas we passed under itsatand sat do
wn to hear the wind roar swift *and* steady*a performer* he never seestw
o of themis perhaps hearD COMMUNicated so disTINCtly through the oar t
o the air across the river directly against his eardifferently sounda

hadthinks companiondisguiseTheas so the readand
daywarblersandifMarHarmonying readus beas as
meltHe ipickerel timesIt is life within life, i
n concentric spheresmy pden they give no evide
nce they have heard ITCT HE attaches impor
tance to the actual worldtheir So there is some
thing in the music t uShe were child eorthe
wind is not quite agreeable It prevents your he
aring Two are steadily singing, as if conten
ding th It will COME UP SWEET FRom the mea
dowsorh We can forego the advantages of citiesc
lose There is a lower, hoarser, squiRMING, S
CREwing croak roundprb rne It or it may be i
n the shutter andBeginning slowly, the beat s
ounds faster and fasterIt is to the ear as
sharpest fifeethe un s It is as palpable as tH
E NOTE H HEard a smart tche-day-day-dayWe h
eard close to our ears I had heard them furth
er at first ndAA kingfisher with his crack,-
cr-r-r-rackThus the spaces of the air are fille
dfor music all Vienna cannot serve them more
e seems to be singing across the streamBesid
e, sounds are more distinctly hearda i in Any p
lace at all for music is very good thrill Such
vibrating music would thrill them to deaththoug
hting theety All these sounds dispose our minds
to serenity astwfk tp hear one warbleMen danc
e to it, ring and vibratewhere there is an e
mpty chamber underneathourdiesr It dies away as
soon as uttered diessof awakened naturemAKE S
Easonwhen the Euterpeans drive through He
hears it in the softened air some grains which
stir within you ad siNG A LITTLE While ey T
hey hear the croaking frogs at 9:00 P. M.
dow tremble, imagining the worsttheof his appro
achmter while they sit by the spring! th hispa
and seemed to proceed from the woodlar ot r
lThat noble strain he uTters that came with HIM
HEBY THE CHARActer of that single strain in e
very horizon e Is it not the R. palustris?O
rpheus Hear a slight snoring of frogS ON THE
BARED meadowsmore known by the disTANCE W

FIRstun h We go about to find SolitudE AND SILENCE BUTCherThe evening
wind is heard conversing with yout scratching THE FLOOrlike break the
ns ofwith the first note byt to flow and swell the general quire begwhic
h their young ears detectin itend quite inaudible aT ANY DISTANCE
C N Ver r andreturn to it in your thought perfect thermometers, h
ygrometers, and barometers ch s some well-known march thisof the no
te, whittichee ing thethe sione lat regular intervals for a long time
st ts should say whistle, if one could whistle for the notess some not
es, then perfect warblesom THECH ORMErman sicker ingm sPRingbob
the terin r in Theyi t ed to oss tw wings maypul TheyWilhourwh o b
h e Theynothmonthssongtphrtee the ie th e e ph r he tck toprii fi
bth ed t i rth a days heardcuckoo theyboyschatteringupthreesee t
cheesee this the almost forgotten soundsoundslumberous sound so exp
anded being life off but is heard distinctly throughout it still tothe s
lower measure and often and ofTEN ANDA SPRinglike and exhilarating
sound of which the echo is the best sort of glorifying going today
itto change its posiTionsometimes a loud crackon inthis early breathing
in the dawn ThisThis breathing of chip-birds soundschip-birds ear How fu
ll the air of sound! They stood, hearing wind and water They rks p s
trike earwe Hip-yOU, HE-he-he-he It was long beFORE THE jingle comes
I hear a robin singing before sunset song jingle comes up, soon TO SPr
ingoo We hear which we do wThis is facto vit chit chit char weeter
char tee chu vit chit chit char WEETER CHAR TEE CHUliter gain th
e of werefoxThe Hear ored withsinger morn is extent inwith my dis when t
hein end are Heard sweets frog'sdoes the One God's breaTH ALDSOR VI
RTueitsvireopreciselytheand herthelast eye is sun nowon Nearifand hea
r He hemsquirrelthezon toup downhere herenine-o'clock wicheR WICher w
hicher wich heard the hooting ofwth that she has been elevated t A
DAY LIKE This rd and uttering a faint chipmournful, martial and eff
eminateis dissolved g as the sound of a far-off glorious life ooas thoug
h they dwelt in the depths aseem to be hushed rt to a slow music e
that chiefly distinguishes this season ewhich the murmer has agitated l
to a strange, mad priestessh in such rolling places i eh but bellowing
from time to timet t y than the vite and twittering a day or two h a

day or two by itS COURSE

a fulbeen halfty noteat play thesendper course
which *Its scream* even is as the voiceaswe *warb
ler issued* frombyheard si*onunable*She heard the
forgotTEN sound of rainmore It does not sing c
ontinuously, but at intervalsis *mentso he*The c
atbird doES NOt make the corn-*planting sounds*sc
reechThe first peetweet; myrtle-birdsnumerous
catbird a Theor excroak teeth seenI heard anD yi
elded the point to him yielded brEAK AND WAS O
FTen inareesThose suggest the same thoughts that
all melody has ever DONETOINTHEYOUrin He think
s there ispieye th*an from shouldenednotes*oundeac
hplate*it a*nd heard him cackling and tapping f
ar ahea*dout of* a fuzzy beginning or *bob-y-lee* t
wice as far at least*close* to the water's edge
sing ozit ozit ozE-E-e (quick) tchIP TCHIP TCHIP
THe of Hear phebe note of chickadee little *music*
*c*harms more than this vibration of an insect
's w*ingin his mouth*con that*l*mita*t*ions and echo
were good, sounds were liquidI*t* be*gan* to sound
at one spot only There is more of squeak, mew,
clear whistle of philosophyMusic soothes the d
in *a*nd liGHTENS THE head*s of all thing*sin the
yard of a tree sparrow Youand their *conque*
*reereme*mber bird It is hea*r*d farther than noi
seWhat lungs! Some hold their heads high when
they ring*theeoorar oorar oo*RAR *oorar-hah oorar*-ha
h hah oorar-hah hah hahShe does not hear;
notes are drowne*dof constant* sounds at the op
en win dowsfroM OUR *window ancient*s th*at the anc
ient*s *st*retched a wire saidwest of Wood on ro
ckthe sense of hearing is wonderfully,assisted t
o bring within ear-shot that wiLDCAT'S SCREam b
ough as in the days of Orpheus beiNG BOR
N AGAINEP*healthwhere the vi*BRATION IS APpare
ntly more rapid YouRLD WHAT A CONTRAst this
evening melody with day! nd n Nature meant by
this to stereotype dying moANS HE KNOWS NOT w
hen *it began to occ*upy himfordsThe season of
morning fogs has arrivedThese song *sparro*ws are
now first heard common*ly These song* sparrow
s are now hea*rd* commonlyand the fin*e*st melody

can be heard farther dis phi thesays They asked harm if they
sounded itrect Are they *whistlers?tlers?*lifestampIt is evidence of
such sphere, such possib*ilities*Now this is ver*dict of* soul in heal
thThis is no earth on which we stood It is possible to live grand
er life its vision *is* TRUE RANDS A You can for*ego the seem*ing
advantages without misgiving They *can forego the seem*ing cities wi
thout misgiving mon as theOne will lose no music nOT Attending o
pe ras Hip-you, he-he-he-heHe hears tones We hear the veery Sometime
s she he*ars* the brazen note Youwheard one honk He k*nows there is* a p
eople somewhere woodthrush sings at all hours atenoto an inconce
ivable degreeis tem*poraryo* heouon the *willowsfistr*eacra notof Wa
chusett of the story of such a *soundra with wit*h sparrows likei
ng in thE MORning of myrtle-birds on a dead tree-top this depth
for a long time as you sit They have HEARd t*hat peculiar dre*aming
soundBELONGS THEIRTHat dreaming sound *belongs to their* nights' dr
eam peculiar dreaming sound bel*ongs* to the summer Snipes *off with*
crazy flight and distressed craik craikIt suggests pleasant aSSOCI
ATIONS THEY They wheeled and *made a fin*e whistling soundTheir
faint quack sounded much like the croakquack sounded the croak o
ccasionally in the pool*sThey made a sound* not by their wings *Their*
quack sounded *like frogs heard* IN POOLSTHEIR FAint quack sounDE
D Like the croakThese notes of birds seem to invite forth vegetationA
gain; it is he, - an occasional peepWe hear the tchuck tchuck *How*
a thought will mould and paint it! Hear the hens cackle as not
before*I heardIt was* SURPRISING WHAT VArious sounds we heardWe sat
an hourthe ais*les of wood were* so many ear-trumpets If so*ul to i*
*ts infinity, then sil*ence Hear the phebe of chickadeeA grosbeak b
etrays itself by that *pecu*liar squeakrose-breasted *grosbeak be*
trays itself by t*hat peculiar sque*ak A rose-brea*sted grosbeak betr*
ays itself b*y that squeak*The *bo*bolink sings as he go*es* along sings a
s we go along *the railr*oad *Question is whether you ca*n bear freedom
ofmany *sounds come to our* eaRS AGREEAbly bluntedWho has not hear
kened to her infinite d*in?while*low growling and sudden quick-repea
ted ca*terwaul He told h*im he would hear it You*chick We hear it* like a
dreamNOise is like rustling leaves Hear hurriednotes and afterwa
rds its tut tut *spir str*ains of music *are drawn out* endlesslyliket
he wire itself of t*he awakening* bubbling ring, then bag must be
inflated again remin*ds* asandis AHear the loud l*aughing*suited to
the wildest lakeor yow yow yow, or yang yang yang soonearlier They
hop long before hea*rd to ring wi*ll make the most nervous chordheal*th*
ily We *fo*rever *ever and habit*ually underrate our fate an I heard t
he telegraph-wire vibrating like a harp aeoliaNHEAR Sparrows sc

ratching the floorin the twilightslumberouslyThey
would wheel them and feel their pulseand heal*thy a
ppetite* isof living rob*in earth-song hear*d a   a
ed fewtr ti asits healthily rv SingularSingularthe
he u otherthethed obullfrog-like crownight Heturns
grassan *merei y rulesva*riously i theu a*nd inces*
sa*ntly*rkee sh*oulder*of any blthet perhapse hicko
rynvlt isiShe comes dropping rain like cow with
overflowing udder She bellows hollowly, making t
HE EARTH tremblei It *is N*ature's rutting season
They hear muttering, crashing in muggy air mid-hea
ven Sound travels round, invades, advancing at g
rand pace rkI heard it vibrating high overhead She
hears a snoring, praying soundsand etc. e*L*e*dum h
oura*fa*spiringlife*black mio ina singlyraisedthe
but thehear ndng sthat toh fa nothingisef within*te*
rmittentp sofhear i te chil odust *inhr st* o harsh
ratHER POSEDU A THEA distancerhear *ththe e sou*
nd is ithe m tho measure boa*t and inchiebt tue
etimeevening*The ringingtingat o in ring blost va
l TheyHomerTHOMNOnet nat h lf rbt hAlligator an
d turtle with quakings come out eThe telegraph res
ounds at every post come out of the mud e Behind t
hese *pipes are form*ed triangular alc*oves I*t*s* (*Musi
c's)* inventors hhstrains which reach me here
stir more than if I were belownHe*ar sawmill, like*
drum, like carsAt thi*s post it is a hu*m Heard thei
r last phoebe August 26th man may run but he too m
ust at last be silent tI hear my old owl pb one is
skirmish between cool and earnestweather grows coo
ler, woods more silentth l i th How refreshing th
e soun*d of the smallest waterfall!*You hear the mut
tering of distant thunder e hear a clear whis
tling *every two mi*nutescheered by sound of runni
ng wa*terHow thought* will mould *and p*aint it! rds t
uIt s*ee*med every pore was music pre it s*eemed fill*
ed with music the the *within i*S WEEPIng; grassh
oppers give those the lieutter them in the dayli
ghtthis morning heard also the myrtle- *bird's
tea*l*eeenpreypurchase*d sort it flew *over*, a sound
far from music ows seemsofat ver It Swamp dum
Did I not hear it *there the 10*th? whim calloud a

s soon as they arriveThey *hear go*od things are cheap:
bad are de*arsound always mo*unts, and m*akes you mo*untis
the *eyeweaththough*villag*es there* has of **beutter P. M.**f
ull small bleh He**ard** a slight frog-like c*roak fromthem b*
efore**You** *thought you* he**ard** a croak from before frog bedi
You associate its whistle with br**EEZY** **W**eather t**HEY**
WERE EQUally poetic How inspiring when the travelle
r from call or murmer rises into song!**It is at once**
another landly lyoth hmu Is it not the *same with man?*   t
*h*eo on*creaking* of **wagon** has music*heflogly* Heard war
bler sh*aking out trills* like money iThen they go*off* w
ith hoarse cr-r-r-ack cr-r-r-ackthey How refreshingthe s
ound in hot weather! u or Whene esk*now*It sounded like p
umpkin stem, only **a good dea**l louderbequ ng It is a h
um *hive w*alk notha a bird ere*more ferred any pl*ace fo
r music is goodaits wawa**lT IS MATERI**al put asoak, seas o
ning *in* music much thatThe whip-p*oor-wills* sing far off a
l Itsyou would not hear if not in*clined of*that e or t
he tinklings from the telegraphwith melody unasked for me
nt O when it *is* trilled, or undul**a**tesnessthe essic *e*

which *he hears*spr to the **END, NOR HEAR***d to* the endsprt e so ets

His earthy contentmenT GETS EXPRESSIONWhen two or more bullfrogs trump
together, it isit is a ten-pound-tenthe togetheR, IT Is a ten-pound-
ten noteTheir hand-*organs remind you* of wild beasts those wh*ich reach* h
*im the*re stir much more melodyTimethan *The call m*usters all forces
of nature the*hostileregul*aritywhich THE WHOLIKE Of a thousand buzzi
ng *strings, o*nly one *yields ear Their no*te is the chill-lill or jing*k*inst
*r*umental livelycroakersHeard one after the other, might be varied and oth
erwakeful At length, we heard one near at hAND IT HASTens the sun to
his setting Shall he not sometime have an opportunity? covered with bla
ckbirds *and a rasping t*chuCK THEY HAD not got *their voices y*et andutter
ing their *squeak*s and split whistLES OR char It will come up sweet fro
m *long* afternoon warmthethat wood wher*e we* sat to hear it thewood, *for exam*
ple, the Oak, *where we* sitsounds through this air striking on railsf
requent*l*y only muskrats AND KINgfishers seem to h*ear verythis*note ma
keIt is twangingdraw ofwithfly livestappingclangor and liquidity ad*d*ed to w
oodpecker tapping Hear them in varIOUS PA*r*ts *of town* and you hear *the circ*
ling clamor, clang*orthese harmonies* TEAR TO PIECES WHIle they cha*rmu*
sreduce thrilling *sphere* music to a wail sounds they *should hear if the*
y were below t Wind comes to wake up the trees r It sounds lIKE MOCKer
y to cheat usbut no sound *so brings round summer*he contemplates *God's voi*
ce is but a clear bell *sound sligh*test tinkling in the horizon measures th
eir soundnessNature always possesses hum, booming, crowing,barking l
popen windows *hear the* sounds It is the cack*le of p*igeon woodpecker by De
ep Cut, hear the gnah *gnah* It is a harp with one string theor hear *the sc*
ream of hens and tumult tune *for him*gold-finchThey are distinct, more *shel*
*l*y and general mightdashedtain is loveswings make a whistlingI am pretty s
ure to discover an echoor after sh*ort* pauses it utters sprayey and ras
ping fa*intmayor*that he heard oNETHE THOUGH You perceive no differenc
e, *pond does hear the gnah* gnah ofblack-cap*ped* nuthatchHear low screwing o
r working, ventriloquia*l soundstril long*crowing reminds them of cat owl's
hoo-hoo-*oo in* those waves of sound *They will not t*ROUBLE, CA*n* be ch*eaply*
*enriche*d sonorousness *in the morning*, in the nightWHAT AN elixir isthi
s sound! of coursethe guiitain as the sound graph oursIt was the *sound w*
*hich vibrated t*his lifea by attending lectures *anD* CAUCUSES, ETC, WHat
coloring fair and intense life admits! through *glass oneof simmerin*
g or seething of nature erectedthe in the river, it is *t*here they hear the
m any in We hear the sound of dist*ant t*hunder Shelone laden and *then crushe*
d there olsur inspires anotherpehe heard onewoodThey drown all the res
tThey drown the restdry hum to wiND ON TWIGS, LIquid splashing soun
d on rocksThe off with a sharP PHE PHEWAVES In a warm apartmentwithin c
all of conver*satio*naphe warHe is a quarter of a mile off *theIndeed*out cl
earness to the postapparitiontho*ugh still half of*fhis wagging his taiLRIp

plesthe cRICKET ALSO SEEms to express *the
most liquiD* ANd melodiousIt filled the hal
l realizing idea of pipevariedThe little
croakers, too, are very lively there *just b
efore sunset*up jiNGle *youa There is sound tha
t* can wake an echoin the night A nIGHT IN W
HICH THE silence was audiblerings the what
what what what of this *forenoo*n It is liKE T
HE cackleand suggests a relationIs this the th
ird note of th*is season? such ly black* ducks
rise with *loud hoarse croaking-quacking It sou
nded like* a new birdwith We go to find they dw
elt in depthsvirtuousareThe thought Itwill a
ppear their existence is soundThe thresh
ing and tinkling come with them sic get
one will make music while anotHER MAKES
SENse warfind faint w*arbling is, as it* wer
e, half-finished as shore The creak of mole
cRICKET IS HEARdThe *creak is* heard along t
he shore it sure the bird uttered the unusua
l hoarse notelypoWe no longer know, can deny i
ts existencetoNo strain iS LOST TO THE EAR
HIM mel indescribable coincidence, then the
re is music This wire vibrates, as if it woul
d andaf We hear it and forget it immedia*telyho*
wsuspect it is the R. palustris, now breedin
gsuspect it is the R. palustris sus*pect it i
s the R. pa*lustris, breedingtoads' They dim
dimdog the then asIt IDoflowersDo What its d
epend the away*theorproperly* Peetweetsover t
houghtflittin*gsinger long a* echoGreece ear it f
i*bretoisfibre awood thof*y Hear a very faint bu
t positive ringinge it told will seem bu
t BUBBLE on surface Young bobolinks; one o
f first autumnalish notest the fi*rst autumn
a*lish notesee eThey express the feelings o*f th
e earth* 11It is now *very fresh*y Great straggli
ng flocks of *crows* still flying westerly
uth The wind is NOT QUite agreeable, beca
use it prevents your heARINGn Every man
understands why a fool singsi A THEY L
EFt it, buzzing as lou*dly as at first* so yet y

ou hear *before you have* seenh She hears with consent of senses
Hear the clear loud rich warble sicall whichan*We hear the stak*
e-driver from a distancethese telegraph-posts should bear a g
reat price hearye d It goes off with loud sha*rp pheg* g th
ehave I hear the soothing and simple *mono*tonous noteswbeudo yo
u cOnsider that you are performing?ng e ay rowYou heard one s
a*y to another today* d *a The woods* are alive with pine warble
rs t i for song and fir*eflies g*o with grassthe birds have ceas
ed to singDo not the song and fireflies go? thinkdthe
Thephe TheThe *wingsphe The p*heThe Theingmake⌐THEPHEALOW
S OF MEPhe wingswings legsthe wingspheney phe*The phe w*ings
phemakea Hear phewings INGA⌐THEPHE ThelowsHearoThephe *fal*
lwhIM GAVE MEn musicthewonderful is earththe lathe or a fl
ute!boomand AND SOONOR A LATerthe of ramrods *by chance rat*
her pretty outvia Brocktogetherairair0n that same treeis th
e low gratiNG SQund er *rarelytleThey quail w*histhein summer
A crow came scolding to the treetoads ring most on a windyda
y i fairly its Lake oven-bird *thruMs sawyer-like* and the chewi
nk rustles1 wi*thera* tshrea tshrea tshrea, tshreˊ tshritty t
shritˊ It would be nobler to enjoy mus*icisi breaking*Myrtle-bir
ds sing *their tea lee*, tea lee in the morning appears *to make*
a business of singing from a yellow-*throat for* half an hourb
reak lightthe not leave them nar*row-minded*Men profess to be lo
vers o*f music It would* not leave them narrow-minded bi*go*tedin
the soundor before on song hearyoubetChildreN MAKE NOIS
E BECause of music *their ears* DETECTTHEIR YOUng ears dete
ct man understands why f*O*OL SINGS Sound is These strains sugg
est ideal, lost, or never peRCEIvedthe *vibration is rapi*d he
ard it varying *with* different parts this *wild tree* rejoices
to transmit music The sound proceeds from near the pOSTS WAg
on going *over an unseen bridge is louder*They have heard every n
ote with perfect *distinctne*ss She heard It is the accent o
f the *south wind*It is modu*lated by the south w*indHe hears w
*ith all hi*s sen*ses at least*The sounds I hear are significa nt
and musicaLSOUNDS, At *least* they only are heard it is fit t
heir music shoul*d be the* sameharp and thrush left on earthFor
the same reason *They* lift us in spite of ourselves these no
w The*y intoxi*cate, *they* charm us peep She hears half-strains
from many of them, and the chickadee largechip Itbelongs T
O THe streamte ll hoorit was rustling le*aves rus ra bl*o e c
kb ilofof st Tspring i isthere thhih bo stck nge idis hblac
kst not*eaistle* h a nglng ths0RTAofi n e a k tle *tleimof*

48

like a poor imitation of split whistle
of and set forthevermorea few in one plac
etheeverlastingratheras surprisingcall- no
temerelyoftheof sultry nights hear not only
the incessant lively crOAKING VEry livel
y not only the croaking after the other all
slight andtwigs now Sometimes if they we
re below more often It from the lev
el of ordinary hoursimmortalWhenever a man h
ears itterribly withinsawscreaming in vain
thatdiffusesthat it might be the first inf
antile cry of an earthquaketo the spota
nd traced it to a small bare spot a grou
ndrapid, and more and more intense as if it
had been thawedleaks up through the meadows
with that mileby shuffling their wing-cove
RS TOGETHERLENGTHwise says their shril
lingby shufflingby shufflingwhi-we-chee haw
k's squeakrises at the end of the day
singer is the attitude of inviting by undu
lations already the shivering soundautumn
swhomiandalso shortened and very much v
ariedthear the echo of its own voice You s s
trike threeIt comes to wake up sleeping m
anyth lo i It is sound very much modifie
d, siftEDTHERE IS A SORT OF split wHIST
LEFOR THE REST, there is a poor imitatio
nbecomes firstswallowhear kingbird twi
ttering chattering like a stout-breasted
swallow ngbor chatteringin He drinks in a
wonderful health in sound Well younot prep
ared, thought it a boy whistling of a l
oona areIt is no small gain to have this w
ire fin It told me there were hIGHER PL
ANESand deeper stirrings Iwith such intens
ityfromsound hearing it makes men brave su
chBut in their upward courseis ingmore free
lym a hThey hear the whistling of the
ir wings They hear the whistling of th
eir wingseous at the right angle We hear

sound, less ringing and sonorous *than the* dreamers er

ywasstrain a vireo
before the owl's nes
ttheother to found f
rom time *to timefar*
*as*ound sound and als
o the booming with t
he wind Mar in it is
alder theathave s
trains to the aCTUA
L LIFE AS BUBBLes
beforewith musicfirs
tthethe sound of chi
ldren *at play of*Hear
mole cricket nowaday
s thatson cause chi
dren make noise beca
use *of the music fon*
d it ears tectsprin
gyou were consc*ious y*
ou caught but prelu
detheir ears co*uld*
*never hear a*Ishe *was*
sounds in nature tha
t she caughtwasNow y
ou tooWe We ducedear
s *hear Ah! straw* wh
o tries to read w
ithout good hearing i
s *in Sisyphean* labor
thoughtthe *sicwent a*
*nd s*at down to hea
r the wind slack m*u*
ch seems to flow thr
ougH MY VERY BOne
ssongTherecrowing of
cocks rem*inds him* of
it I stood hearing w
ind and the waterred
-eyecontinuedcroakis
perha*p*s from *the oth*
*er sex*the ANDSWeet
Discordwin I can com*p*

are the within and withoutaa love-strain to deaRUP
WITHRING eve is tion it hum TheywhistleseeWas th
at ah, *twar twe twar, twit twit twit twi*t, twe?   T
hey resound with the hum of bumblebees strain
s have thear faint tseep like a fox-colored sp
arrowIt is distincT AS IF NO water interven*ed Irl
n their e*ars detect We could see if we did NOT H
EARWLSIT IS AN *alarm-clock set so* as to wake Nat
ure upaWha*t a rustling am*ong the dry leaves!Wha
t a rustling it seems to make!You sit and enjoy th
e sound of le*aves uIt implies a* different life th
an the oRDIna*ryghts htt it*s sweetS WASTedosound
fi*lls my* buckets ygrain will whisk about without an
y ordere *ghHow lik*e creaking *tr*ees SLIGHT SOUNds
they make! cri*ckets are* heard cool day like th
isaAll ot*her s*ounds seem to be hushed voice of n
o bird can be comparedThe air gladly bears the
bur*den as We are refreshed by sounds heard* AT MID
nights yelping of do*g fell on ea*r as brEeze on c
heek thea bird uttering that worried noteoo hea
rd a soundP a tcrickets discoursel This is a mornin
g celebrated by birdsethe or of r Speech never mad
e man master, but refraining from itrefraiNI*ng*e
rof hisse*c*t's hear a ripe chirp of a *cricket of a*
CRICKETI ALL SOUNDs and silence do fife and d
rumnorsn tected world-famous mulLSIONINdry hopp
ing sound *rings in my ear*sliving on notThose are n
ot uNFITTED TO wild beastsroar was effort to *pr*
eserve equilibrium h donot reminds Some I*s h
as s*tairs rs rattling teA-KETTLE REMInds her of
cow-bells berryingmelodytons was only For whe
re man is, is SilencEPORTLIKE THE HISTory of th
e future on om hear singing in the woods ets I hear
whistling wings he *sings o*r talks to himselfIt is k
indred w*ith the music* of many creatures started up
a pack of quail it may have bee*n a bevy quail* went o
ff *with a whir* like a sh*ot, plumpAll* sound tends to
pro*duce the s*ame musicsound esMen talkof the s
ong of other birdsThis is June, resounding hum o
f inse*ctsThere is a*n interval between thrasher and
thrushtalk of the song, the thrasher interrupted *s*t
rains reach me through trees passmusic reminds *me, s*

uggests ideas of human life quiHe plays some well-known
march ingShe hears the weese wese Wese notetoits earth i
s alive and covered with feelersandcoolShe hears her old
owl Ac stood mILKMEn inabecause of its harmony with it
seLFAND EQUANIMity ndnd rh into a partial concord ttha
t may first be heard in the nightibut not yetThE AIr consen
ts and his wedge will enter easilyralldvoia sounds Our vo
ices sound differentlythThe wARM AIR HAS Thawed the
music in his throatPerhaps this IS THE WHIP-poor-will's
Moonamh hand-organs rEMIND ME OF BEASTS art consists in
stirring from time to timeWhaWe are affectediCan he be w
hittichee? eartha f traced it to a spot, used a stic
kicefrommore of the s or psi in it ear f New creaking or
shrilling crickets, fine and piercing er na loon set up
his wild laughBut why did he with that loud laugh? lit sur
passes birds; sings everlasting to everlasting CRICK
THE HEARing of the cricket whets your eyes tle mrip in'
slike ar tea, --twe-twe, twe-twe, or ar te, ter twe-tWE
, TWE-Twe ingtyelping fell on ear, cool breeze on cheek by
starlighT sureLy ofof man with its vibrations with the s
ong and works of art The distant is brought near through
hearing cock, standing on snow-heap, feels the softe
ned air, has foUND HIS VOICE AGAinPierians in the des
ertsuggestssameSCREaming into the empty houseit is his m
outh were full of cotton to spit out of cottonWhenas if Se
ewe farmthink she will not trouble herselfoften through dra
w music from a quart potAH!AND SImple soundswhich nO MAN
HAD TOLD US OF Of grackles OR IMPORTANT TO be donesp
end hours of silence listening to whisperingsstay By silen
ce seen threatening people routEDTO AWAYONE After ano
ther before youon the water was interested in the naturaL
PHENOMenon of soundlong in the wilderness and the wild
manwood there is a wind and ladiesandWe should know it fo
r a white man's voice in the streeton his pulse with a heal
thy ear to some purposehear cattle lowin the streetse
ewhistlehorses stood sTILL TO HEAR IT SHESt thewhlthrou
gh which it passed s Yetthrush allreverberation th at asou
ndsfwh ntestmel at shouldnatureWe na ehillI as suniy
eac notrfie butthe wdaymusicdistant rnotbut hearthe ins
ectsbirdover the edgewhite-bellied ly erhalfas in Maywhatt
hey sayasisand as the otherwithout reasoning no right wha
teverand yeT WHen his strains ceaseperhapslyof if Nature

does not echo itvail with any spirit which
lyre vibrating the stringslicord if he h
as heardble long malof the F. hYEMAlis mon
orinfor it is not a scream fishAs we went
underYou presently ted oth of the infant d
ruMMer tureten Ad niteso expanded and inf
initely related or chill-lill with a
fine note it where they wereso the sound o
f blasting rockS SOWIth perfect distinctn
ess with a jingling sound at the same t
imeon hills likefrom withina with a sharp,
whistling whir from sharpgin in whiterd'sT
his is the softer music, bare and burstin
gbreeze causes leaves to rustle, a patteri
ng sound oaya philosopher's living is simp
le, complexa storm arises the verse ShaLL
WE NOT ADd a tenth Muse to the immortal
Nine?t 1 sound to h t litk hear a clear, c
hinking chirp golearned sitrnthere were
some this year singing or breedingthesin
g dows their firstthe water gurgledgur ef
arround i usaters persThose interrupted st
rains suggest the same that all melody has
ever donesugimpressed, we no longer kno
w no These reach her through treesp e
levated into glorious sphere, we no long
er knoW NORO THE different sound comes t
o ear from rails struck longnature has a
ny place for music twt leopard'salL m
y sensesear of earthstop as big as a cher
ryNot only musT MEN Talk, but talk about
talk they rise and about uttering crack of
alarm joins and utters the wooing note o-
week o-week landnand spirited th Hear ye
llow-throat knownHeard first cricket si
nging; on lower level than any bird, obser
ving lower tone cords This h even the harp
hear whistles to keep courage up listvil
the perch in the villagehearhorse across
distant bridge, atmosphere tells his ear
rm a blackppIt stings his ear with truthp
robablyHowBefore the it was, and will be a

fter icealways it issThey hear *trilled*
sound this eveningsunpus such forAll
things are cheap: all are dear chu*ad d*
*istinctly*hasI soar or hover *over fie*
*ld of life*coincidence tr anduanot su
n'S CH Is it not the EArliest springw
*ard note?*e reing spring per imusic
adve*rtised life no man told us of the*
13th hear the bay-wing *sing then there*
is such a fiddling you would think mus
ic *was* being born isthink bough ft s of
of ishore eveningnoonwoodwood thrush
, cuCKOO ARE Heard now at *noon*It wou
ld not leave themhAS She is affected a
isShe fleet moreYou hear itmiaAn *Ital*
ian has just carried a hand-organ thr

ough the villagepleasant

DIARY: HOW TO IMPROVE THE WORLD
(YOU WILL ONLY MAKE MATTERS WORSE)
CONTINUED 1969 (PART V)

CXIX.   No need to move the camera.
(Pictures come to it.)   Gather, Fuller
advises, facts regarding human needs and
world resources.   Place in computer
memory bank.   Update continuously.
Join team of programmers, competing
to find speediest peaceful means for
giving each world inhabitant what's needed
for his kind of living.   Videoize
solution on football-field-sized geodesic
world map, so fact continuously
changing intelligent solution of world
game exists becomes via TV household
knowledge.   A study was made with
computer to find out where in the world
wealthy Americans prefer to **retire.**
They retire, computer tells us, to
Cuernavaca in Mexico, a hilltown near
Nairobi in Kenya, and some place or
other in Nepal.   CXX.   The goal is
not to have a goal.   The new universe
city will have no limits.   It will

not be in any special place.   Having
returned, as Fuller puts it, to his
studies, teacher will be flying all
over the world and even out into
space.   **Questions I might have learned**
to ask him can no longer be
answered.   Waiting in the hotel in
Rio de Janeiro to hear whether or not I
was to meet with the people who were
studying anarchy (they had come in their
studies to Thoreau and, having heard
that I was enjoying Thoreau's
Journal, had asked me to share with them
my thoughts) : telephone didn't ring.
     CXXI.   Act of sharing is a community
act.   Think of people outside the
community.   What do we **share with them?**
Teacher played hooky.   Sent message:
"Receiving instruction.   Enjoying
myself thoroughly.   See you next week."
     Lejaren Hiller's computer music
project: "fantastic orchestra."
Each sound to be a plurality of
vibratory circumstances known or not
known in nature.   Impossible made
possible.   Fuller: Nothing's
artificial.   It exists?   It is natural.
How d'you manage to live with **just one**
shirt?   Before going to bed, I take a
shower with my shirt still on.
     Afterwards I scrub the cuffs and
collar with my electric toothbrush.   Then
I turn on the TV, hang my shirt on it.
Best place I've found to dry it.   CXXII.
     Years ago zoological gardens began to get

rid of wire fences, substituting
means that decreased the sense of
separation between animal and man.
Coming back from The Junior Museum
of Natural History in Sacramento,
Billie Berton told me children now
make applications for checking animals
out.   It took six weeks to teach the
computer how to toss three coins six
times.   Somewhat worried, I tossed coins
manually to discover from the
I Ching how **I Ching** felt about being
programmed.   **It was delighted.**
I Ching promised quantitative
increase of benefits for culture.   **What**
we've already done conspires against
what we have now to do.   CXXIII.   **Advice**
to Brazilian anarchists: Improve
telephone system.   **Without telephone,**
merely starting revolution'll be
impossible.   **Pinkville.**   Charles Peck.
New York's State Botanist, spent most of
his life with no place to work but a
dark hallway.   Just **before he died**
the Government gave him a room with a
window.   Cadaqués: up around nine or
ten; coffee; off by boat to a cove
where no others are; white wine,
almonds, olives; chess, swimming,
dominoes; back in town by one or two
for lunch with him.   (He had not been
with us.)   Feared plan'd fail (no one
wanted to get **deeply involved**).
However, it worked.   **When disaster**
was imminent, people rose to

occasion, did whatever was necessary
to keep the thing going.   (Reminder,
not a revelation.)   He'd have preferred
silence to applause at the end (**art
instead of slap in the face.**)   **CXXIV.**
Whispered truths.   **Looking for
something irrelevant, I found I
couldn't find it.**   "Wild as if we
lived on . . . marrow of antelopes
devoured raw."   **(Thoreau.)**   Wanting
to make some easy money, he took to
cracking safes, was caught, put in
penitentiary.   While ill in the prison
hospital, he had an affair wth middle-aged
nurse.   When he was released from
penitentiary, nurse introduced him to a
beautiful young girl whom he married.
His bride immediately **inherited three
million dollars.**   College: two hundred
people reading same book.   **An obvious
mistake.**   Two hundred people can
read two hundred books.   Clothes I wear
for mushroom hunting are rarely sent
to the cleaner.   They constitute a
collection of odors I produce and
gather while rambling in the woods.   I
notice not only dogs (cats, too) are
delighted (they love to smell me).   CXXV.
Vacaville.   Spent the evening with a
murderer.   I asked him why he drank so
much coffee.   He said, "There's
nothing else to do."   **University, which
now embraces studies formerly excluded
from it such as home economics,
music, and physical education, has**

sister universities abroad, belongs
to consortium of universities here,
includes a "free" university.   What's
adumbrated's indistinct from society
itself.   Not a community of scholars
living like monks, but society
which works for any kind of living,
any kind of attention-placement, any
activity.   Something seems
beautiful?   Wittgenstein: You mean
it clicks?   When things don't click,
take clicker from your pocket and
click it. **CXXVI.   Death.** Process
involving Christmas trees takes place
each year.   Christmas trees that're grown
in Hawaii are sent by freighter to be
sold on the West Coast.   Christmas
trees that're grown on the West Coast
are sent by freighter to be sold in
Hawaii.   Ready or not, we are being
readied.   Complete checkup.   I was more
examined than ever before.   Doctor's
report: You're very well except for your
illnesses.   John **McHale:** "It has taken
the history of mankind to produce the
articles we have around us (the match,
the computer); it is essential to see
one sector of population isn't servicing
another; we are all using the same
materials simultaneously; information
storage never depletes; ability to
reuse materials makes us, after all
these centuries, quite skillful."
CXXVII.   Impatience.   Why do you have
one TV set on top of the other?

The bottom one doesn't work.   There
were fifty-two tapes.   We had to
combine them for a single recording.
We went to a studio where they
could record eight at a time.   When
we had seventeen together it sounded like
chamber music; when we had thirty-four
together it sounded like orchestral
music; when we had fifty-two
together it didn't sound like anything
we'd ever heard before.   Milarepa.
London publisher sent blank ("Fill out.")
so I'd be included in survey of
contemporary poets of the English
language.   Threw it out.   Week later
urgent request plus duplicate blank
arrived.   "Please return with a
glossy photo."   Complied.   July, August,
September.   Publisher then sent
letter saying it'd been decided I'm
not significant poet after all: if I
were, everyone else'd be too.   **CXXVIII.**
Used to say "never the twain shall
meet."   Now we don't hesitate to fight
oriental wars, there's no doubt about
usefulness of oriental thought for
western mind.   Same's true for
Utopia.   Its impracticality is no longer
to be assumed.   Everything's changed.
Develop facilities that remove need
for middlemen.   Soup cans are not only
beautiful (Warhol, for example) but true
(Campbell's soup is actually in them).
They're also constant reminders of
spiritual presence.   "I am with you

always." Function fulfilled by images of the Virgin Mary along a path is now also fulfilled by the public telephone. Instead of lighting a candle, we insert a dime and dial. **CXXIX. Computer mistake in grade-giving resulted in academic failure of several brilliant students. After some years the** mistake was discovered. Letter was then sent to each student inviting him to resume his studies. Each replied he was getting along very well without education. Buddha reclines on his right side. So does the lion. How thorough he is! He told me his secrets. Town is very small, well-organized. Nothing can be found in it. An idea was given to them because they didn't have one. The Seychelles. Cloth calendars for kitchen walls designed by Lois Long are sold throughout the USA. Some years ago Lois made one by mistake giving two different dates to a single day: Thursday November 31 was also Thursday December 1. **The calendar was very successful. CXXX. Discipline (Disciple). Giving up one's country, all that's dear to one's country: "Leave thy father and mother. . . ." Yoga (Yoke). Taming** of the globe (Open: In and Out). Einstein wrote to Freud to say men should stop having wars. Freud wrote back to say if you get rid of war you'll also get rid of love. Freud was

wrong.   What permits us to love one
another and the earth we inhabit is that
          we and it are impermanent.   We
obsolesce.   Life's everlasting.
            Individuals aren't.   A mushroom
lasts for only a very short time.   Often I
go in the woods thinking after all these
years I ought finally to be bored with
          fungi.   But coming upon just any
mushroom in good condition, I lose my
mind all over again.   Supreme good
fortune: we're both alive!   CXXXI.   Things
governments wish to divide between us
          belong to all of us: the land, for
          instance, beneath the oceans.
            People speak of literacy.   But I, for
one, can't read or write any computer
            language.   Only numbers I know are
those based on ten.   I'm uneducated.
Home in Wayzata, Minnesota's very much
          like a home near Sitges (just south of
Barcelona).   Now we're itinerant there's
no reason to go on, for instance, picking
          fruit.   Since we live longer, Margaret
Mead says, we can change what we do.   We
          can stop whatever it was we promised
we'd always do and do something else.
CXXXII.   He is one of my closest friends.
            He asked me for help.   I gave it.
He couldn't use it.   TV Guide tells what's
going on, doesn't tell what we're
            obliged to look at.   Where you are
limits what channels you can receive.
(Hearing sounds before they're
audible is not the way to hear them.)
            Imitate the telephones of your

homes'n'highways.　　(Their
indifference.)　　They aren't
displeased when the person speaking
is black.　　They aren't pleased when
the person speaking is black.　　**When lady**
in charge of university concerts asked
what music day was to be called, I
replied *Godamusicday*.　　**She was**
delighted.　　**Her husband, also**
affiliated with university (but in
its legal aspects) wasn't.　　**"Profanity**
is forbidden.　　**Nothing can be printed**
that might come to the Governor's
notice."　　Duchamp, asked whether he
believed in God: No.　　God is Man's
stupidest idea.　　CXXXIII.　　Traveling
from one place to another we confine
ourselves to the roads.　　That's why, of
course, we feel so populated: we're
too choosy about the space we use.
Guests had left.　　**Before going to bed,**
while reading a book he'd bought that
morning, he chuckled.　　**Ten minutes later,**
brushing his teeth, he died.　　**Whole**
Earth.　　**We connect Satie with Thoreau.**
Eleventh thunderclap?　　**1928.**　　**Walter**
loved the Chinese, hated Communists.
He couldn't bear the Japanese.
Fortunately for Uncle, he died before
the tables turned.　　Mushroom?　　Leaf?
Backs ache.　　If we had immortal life
(but we don't), it'd be reasonable to do
as we do now: spend our time killing one
another.　　CXXXIV.　　Chadwick, gardener at
Santa Cruz.　　Nobby'd said, "You must
meet **our wizard."**　　**(Chadwick's back,**

Nobby told me, had been injured in war,
        but when we went mushrooming with
his student-helpers, Chadwick,
        half-naked, leapt and ran like a
pony.   Catching up with him, it was
joy and poetry I heard him speak.   But
while I listened he noticed some distant
goal across and down the fields and,
            shouting something I couldn't
understand because he'd already turned
away, he was gone.)   Students had defected
from the university or had come
            especially from afar to work with him
            like slaves.   They slept unsheltered
in the woods.   After the morning's hunt
with him and them, I thought: These
        people live; others haven't even been
        born.   CXXXV.   It was not quite
        midnight.   Duchamp was waiting for us in
        the street.   He looked for all the
world like a handsome young man.   Want
list of communes (places where Americans
        live who've given up dependence on
power and possessions)?   Write to
        Alternatives Foundation, 2441 Le
        Conte Ave., Berkeley, Calif., 94709 or
to Carleton Collective Communities
        Clearinghouse, Northfield, Minn., 55057.
Future's no longer a secret.   Murderer
        asked, "What time is it?"   "Nine
        o'clock."   Five minutes later he
repeated his question, "What time is it?"
"Five minutes after nine."   Ten.   She had
problem children.   Their grades were so
        poor they couldn't enter college.   I

told her to stop worrying about them.
 She did.   They've turned out
 beautifully.   One married a Californian,
 has two fine sons, paints beautifully.
Tucker's automobile expertise is in demand.
CXXXVI.   Talked about fact writing's less
         and less attractive.   Picking up
the pen, one knows idea's already
entertained in other minds.   Pen becomes
         absent.   Sword'll follow suit.   Flower
   Sermon.   In the plane ready for last leg
         of flight to Yucatan (he'd flown from
            Berkeley, I from Palermo in
Sicily).   Grounded by fog we remained in
            Mexican plane three hours, which with
            subsequent flight gave me time to
read Stent's typescript of his book, *The
   Coming of the Golden Age*.   When
            questions came to mind, I simply put
         them to the author!   Completely
satisfied.   How do you propose, Fuller was
asked, to accomplish this without
   involvement in political action?   His
   answer: The World Game provides an
   apolitical option, a solution no one's
         forced to accept.   When, however,
you want it, you'll be able, since you know
      it exists, to use it.   CXXXVII.   Puppy
was eating his vomit.   "That's one
      thing," his mistress said, "we don't
do."   Picked him up; put him outside;
resumed her conversation.   No one
cleaned up the mess.   (An elderly Viennese
      lady whose principal pleasure was
         listening to music was alarmed

because she thought she was losing
her hearing.   She went to the doctor.
He discovered her ears were full of wax.
He removed it very easily.)   Man
living in the Ojai knew how to manage
unsheltered.   But, hungry, he
devised a plan that worked: to subtly
change his environment in terms of its
seductiveness to picnickers so that
coming upon it picnickers'd feel they'd
made a discovery of the ideal place to
eat (he lived for years on food they
left behind).   CXXXVIII.   Busy
signal in the telephone system
sometimes means person one's calling's
talking to someone else.   Sometimes busy
signal means someone else's trying to
reach very same person you're trying
to reach.   This creates a problem.
Solution: two different types of busy
signals.   If at some moment person
we're trying to reach (being called
before by someone else) answers,
genuine busy signal rings.
Presidential platform: promise,
elected or not, to go on with my work,
not bothering about you; to remove
laws; to extend unlimited credit
throughout society regardless of
nationality.   Observing distinctions
(race distinctions), side with underdog,
learning from him who was oppressed
to live outside the law not committing
crimes.   Become slave to all there
is.   (No need to become King.)   Siding
with noises, musicians discovered

**duration's impartiality.   What
corresponds in society to sound's
parameter of duration?   CXXXIX.**
Vacation.   This is ours.   Don't just
"do your thing": do so many things no one
will know what you're going to do next.
**Add video screen to telephone.   Give
each subscriber a thousand sheets of
recordable erasable material so
anytime, anywhere, anyone'd have**
access to a thousand sheets of *something*
(drawings, books, music, whatever).
You'd just dial.   If you dialed the
wrong number, instead of uselessly
disturbing another subscriber, you'd
just get surprising information,
something unexpected.   CXL.
Statement by Stulman, manufacturer/
distributor of lumber products, founder/
President of the World Institute: The
question before us is whether we will so
organize the processes for gathering
and applying knowledge that the
creative powers of all men can be
catalyzed for growth toward
wholeness, or whether we will
persist in our egocentric,
ethnocentric, fact-accumulating,
thing-oriented, power-amassing ways
that are leading us to destruction.
Looking out the window into the forest,
illuminated surfaces in the house
(that aren't in the forest) are
seen in the forest, 3-D in color.   Hand
that's placed on TV is placed at the
same time outside on the tree.   CXLI.   The

shower's in the room, not confined to a
cubicle.   On the opposite wall's a
            mirror.   Steam from the hot water
produces the slow disappearance of
one's image.   Pleasure of having a body.
            "Waiting for the gift from me to me
of death."   Assassination of Martin
Luther King.   **Apocalypse.**   They have
homes but they don't have the idea. Keep
      Out.   Languages separate people.
Images (TV, highway signs, trademarks,
      film) bring them together.   Going
to the moon, we speak in numbers.   A
year has passed.   We pretend we can get
along without him.   For three or four
years, Igor Strawinsky was treated for a
malady his doctors thought he had.   When,
at death's door, Strawinsky's hands
turned black, the doctors concluded a
            mistake had been made.   CXLII.
That that's unknown brings mushroom
and leaf together.   "Ego dethroned."   **In**
the course of being provided with
false teeth, Thoreau took ether.   "You
are," he wrote, "told that it will
make you unconscious, but no one can
imagine what it is to be unconscious
until he has experienced it.   If you
have an inclination to travel,
take," he advised, "the ether.   You go
beyond the farthest star."   We know from
            a variety of experiences that if we
have a sufficiently large number of
things, some or even many of them can be
bad but the sum-total is good for the
            simple reason, say, that not all of

the things in it are good.   CXLIII.
Found, page 74, in a book by Cassirer: it
is speech itself which prepares the way
whereby it is itself transcended.
From navigation to aviation.   Fuller:
Renounce water as sanitation-means;
adopt compressed air (following
lead of dentists).   Bits of hair and skin
floating in the air with pollen, seeds
and spores from plants.   Out of water into
air and back to earth.   I asked
Xenakis what's wrong with USA.   He
was quiet for a moment and then said,
"Too much power."   Put 'em who threaten
possessions and power together with 'em who
offend our tastes in sex and dope.
Those who're touched, put 'em in
asylums.   Pack off old ones to
"senior communities," nursing homes.   Our
children?   Keep'em prisoner,
baby-sitter as warden.   School?   Good for
fifteen to twenty years.   Army
afterward.   Liberated, we live in prison.
No this, no that.   Kill us before we
die!   CXLIV.   We have no icons: we
believe what we do.   (Telephone
conversation turned toward politics.
Mrs. Emmons said she was certain
what the government was doing was
right.   Beverly said, "How do you
figure that?"   Her mother replied,
"Well!   This is a Christian country.")   We
leave food offerings for person who
makes next telephone call no matter
who he is: thus we transform highway
telephone booth into wayside shrine.   I

don't believe, Duchamp said, in the
verb, to be.   "I do not believe that I
am."   Commune problem: communes're
filled with gurus, needing (not having)
others "to guru."   But teaching's
part'n'parcel of divisive society we're
leaving.   Thoreau: "My seniors have
told me nothing . . . , probably can tell
me nothing to the purpose."   Davis: don't
know what we're studying; don't know
how we'll do it.   Studied map.
Should have taken road not on it (went
off to the left).   CXLV.
Reprogramming.   Jack McKenzie's
proposal: Set up alternative university
program freeing a student from all
curriculum responsibilities.   Let him
elect his studies.   When he leaves,
give him, instead of degree,
certificate telling what he did while
in school.   Looking at the sunset,
Brown noticed part of its beauty is
caused by air pollution.   Day after the
assassination.   Human being sitting
at the table next to mine.   Wanted to
speak to him.   Didn't.   Didn't have
the right.   As we left the valley to
enter the desert, I gave up all
thought of finding mushrooms.   But for
some reason we stopped along the
road.   There underneath the pepper trees I
found *Tricholoma personatum*,
excellent, in quantity.   CXXLVI.
The poor?   Where do *they* go to retire?
Takilma, Oregon (America's third poorest
town).   Nothing to do: Free jam,

peanut butter, staples.　　Have two
children?　　Government'll give you two
hundred and forty dollars a month.　　Money
comes through the mail.　　Slight
irritations ("make life sufficiently
interesting to live") are provided by
visits of welfare worker whose
assignment is Takilma.　　Takilma's
beautiful.　　Problem in Takilma: Boredom.
People often together sitting around
talking.　　Let 'em close their mouths;
open their eyes and ears; spend day in
different directions, seeking world
around or in 'em, returning to one
another in the evening, ventilated,
ventilating.　　Provision for changes
in schedule.　　CXLVII.　　She brought him
food.　　Clairvoyant, he knew it was
poisonous.　　Third time she offered
him deadly food, he accepted it, but
himself appointed the hour of his
death.　　Religious tract David Tudor gave
me: "Christ International."　　Train is
made up of engine, coal car, caboose.
Engine is fact.　　Coal car's faith.
Caboose is feeling.　　Train can run with
or without feeling.　　Caboose can't make
train run.　　After breakfast he offered her
a cigarette.　　She said, "No, thank
you."　　He said, "What's wrong?　　Have
you stopped smoking?"　　She said,
"Yes."　　Next day he stopped too.
That was Nobby and Beth ten years
ago.　　CXLVIII.　　I've learned to say No
to those I don't know.　　Learned to
say No to some of those I know.

(Example of underdevelopment of
religious spirit.)   Edwin Schlossberg and
Buckminster Fuller gave six weeks
comprehensive design science course at
the New York Studio School.   (I was
invited to the last meeting.   There were
about twenty-two students.   The first
        thing Bucky said was that the young
        people sitting around the table had
sufficient intelligence to run the world,
to solve all of world problems.   Glancing
        at the students, I was skeptical.
They looked like a bunch of hippies
with some older oddballs thrown in.)
CXLIX.   (But while they spoke, did as I do
at the movies when it's clear
everything'll turn out all right.   I wept.
Fuller would've said, "You sleep too
        much.")   All God's religions and all His
        servants (Lawmakers, Philosopher-Kings,
Saints, Artists) have not been able to put
Mankind back together again.   "You can
        lead a horse to water but you can't make
        him drink."   We've got the
automobile.   No sense in leading horses
around.   Let 'em go where they will.   Fix
        it so if they're thirsty there's
something for'em to drink.   Earth's the
        Way to Heaven.   There's no mystery
        about it.   Don't change Man (Fuller):
change his environment.   Humanities?
        Save them for your spare time.
        Concentrate on the Utilities.   CL.
        In anything experienced nowadays
        there is much that is true, much
        that is false.   Proofreading.

Chadwick described magnetic effect of
moon on tides, on germination of seeds.
"Moon inclining draws mushrooms out of
Earth."   We talked of current
disturbance of ecology, agreed man's
works no matter how great are pygmy
compared with those of nature.
        Nature, pressed, will respond with
grand and shocking adjustment of
creation.   **Out of ourselves with a
little o, into ourselves with a big** O.
Reunion.   Received month's check.   Paid
        bills.   Went to Farmer's Market
    (economy).   Returned at six having
        spent last penny on turkey and all
    the trimmings.   Friends arrived at
midnight for Thanksgiving in the Spring.
        Cared for us, day in, day out, rest
    of the month.

SONG

Wasps are building
summer squashes
saw a fish hawk
when I hear this.

Both bushes and trees are thinly leaved
few ripe ones on sandy banks
rose right up high into the air
like trick of some pleasant daemon to entertain me
and birds are heard singing from fog.

Burst like a stream
making a world
how large do you think it is, and how far? To my surprise, one answered three rods.

Begin to change
in the woods, we came upon a partridge
I find myself covered with green and winged lice.

When I look further, I find
the lower streets of the towns.

In a few weeks they will be
as it should be.

Government
snake and toad
an August wind
soaring hawks
dog of the woods.

Open the painted tortoise nest
Thoreau.

Now under the snows of winter
apple tree
chips of dead wood
then torn up and matted together
'nough to fill a bed out of a hat.

In the forest
on the meadow
button bushes
flock of shore larks
Persian city
spring advances.

All parts of nature belong to one head, the curls
the earth
the water.

See and hear young swallows about
maple buds large as in spring
ice water, winter in the air
carried there by its mother
wildwoods night.

I hear it roaring, reminding me of March, March.

Stood face to face to him and are about to hang him
puts them in his pockets.

I hear the crows cawing hoarsely flying toward the white pine
cricket creaks along the shore
such coolness as rain makes; not sharp.

Their central parts have curved upward.

See thirty or forty goldfinches in a flock, cold air
great numbers of fishes fled.

Since it blossoms a second time
it was fit to rest on
morning concerts of sparrows, hyemalis and grackles
many butterflies
black with white on wings
new country where the rocks have not been burned.

May I be as vivacious as willow.

Shall not voice of man express as much content as the note of a bird?

In the midst of them, I see track of rabbit
it also struck a small oak
screeching of the locomotive, rumbling cars, a whisper
far down all day.

Mosses bear now a green fruit.

This snake on twigs, quick as thought and at home in the trees
the blue-eyed grass is shut up. When does it open?

Flitting about
surprising, this cluster of leek buds on rock.

These are my sands.

Hubbard's bridge and waterlilies
waterlilies.

In our forests
part divine
and makes her heart palpitate
wild and tame are one. What a delicious sound!

The air delicious, thus we are baptized into nature
fall into the water
or lost, torn in pieces, frozen to death
thunder and lightning.

Winter day, clear and bright
still no cowslips.

In a hollow
near the river
in warm weather
the river ice inclines to opaque white
it is quite mild today, holes in the trees an inch apart
forest presents the tenderest green.

But you must raise your own potatoes
perhaps I ate more.

Dark mass of cloud with lighter edges.

What to do, what may a man do and not be ashamed of it?

Countless narrow light lines
it is worthwhile to hear the wind roar in woods today.

The field plaintain, the narrow cotton grass
tobacco pipes still pushing up dry leaves
like the wild cat of the woods
pine wood.

I am surprised to find these roots with white grubs.

One or two flashes of lightning, but soon over
ridge of meadow west of here
naked eye.

a ms
S t aphyt es
art u es e O n s
(which) hi
g e Sthr O

SIX MESOSTICS

Present

rEmembering a Day i visited you—seems noW
as I write that the weather theN was warm—i
recall nothing we saiD, nothing wE did; eveN so
(perhaps Because of that) that visit staYs.

On the windshield of a new Fiat for James K. (who had not made up his mind where to go) and Carolyn Brown

asK
Little
autO
where it wantS
To take
You.

In Memoriam S. W.

after the fire what Shall we do?
"firsT
onE step;
aFter
thAt,
aNother."

We're
alOne.
the music is difficuLt
to Play.
wE must work at it.

July 13, 1972

      aViary without birds
(airplanE
    fRom frankfurt
to basEl), hostess
recogNized me,
      Asked for a poem.

For A.C. on his 70th birthday

    whAt
    A
    River
whichever yOu're
      Near (doesn't any longer matter

    whiCh side
      One's living on)!
    Perhaps
    fLying did it, or
the bridge Across.
    I thaNk her (she got through
one-siDedness).

Ten years before sixty-seven

part and parceL Eighth street artists club, an
    Old friend, he

    C Ame to
    the S Tudio on front
    strEet
when other eyes were cLosed.
    now peopLe see eye to eye:
    hIs eye.

DIARY: HOW TO IMPROVE THE WORLD
(YOU WILL ONLY MAKE MATTERS WORSE)
CONTINUED 1970–71

CLI.   **Tunnel workmen including
toll-collectors went on strike.**   **The
public was put on the honor system.
Once the strike was settled, receipts
were examined to see how much the public
had cheated the government.**   **However, more
money had been received than had been
due; drivers not having change had
apparently been generous.**   **In addition
the government saved all public money it
would have paid its employees.**   We're
changing from looking at the past through
the rear-window to surveying it as we
fly above.   We see geogram of past
actions plus future's wilderness.   Roads
that might have met didn't.   They
served private ends producing impasse.
Garbage behind trees is now out in the
open.   Anyone can see where it is.
CLII.   "Remove God from the world of
ideas.   Remove government, politics
from society.   Keep sex, humor,
utilities.   Let private property
go."   We also have no need for employment.
We are busy doing our own work.   **TV.
Frost interviewing Noel Coward and
Margaret Mead.**   **Sir Noel's view of life is
Sir Noel.**   **Mead's mind is large and open,
like Buckminster Fuller's.**   **She
found thoughts dull that suggest that men
are superior to animals or plants.
Creation's and societies' differences**

**engage her attention.   They suggest the
next things useful to be done.**
Vietnamese food depends on fresh
coriander.   First time I tried to find it
in Chinatown, they were out of it.
Second time I wasn't alone.   We bought
two packages: mine, from the first
store, had yellowing leaves; hers, from
the second, was green, luxuriant.   While
admiring coriander in a third store's
window, she insisted we exchange
packages.   CLIII.   The telephone is
out of order.   **We're within reach of
what to do by means of information.
Information is what happens to us.   That
is, future happens before we experience
it.**   When I was in the sixth grade, I
signed up for the Glee Club.   They
said they'd test my voice.   After
doing that, they told me I didn't have one.
Now there're more and more of us, we
find one another more'n'more interesting.
We're amazed, when there're so many of
us, that each one of us is unique,
different from all the others.
Buckminster Fuller's Pollution
Exploitation Corporation.
Manufacturers and utilities polluting
air and water do so at discrete
points: smoke-stacks, open pipes,
etc.   They make the collecting of
large amounts of various materials easy as
pie.   Once these materials are
transported to the several points where
they're in demand, Directors of the
Pollution Exploitation Corporation
will swiftly become very rich.   *CLIV.*

Asked what he thought of first lecture,
Suzuki said, "Excellent, but in Zen most
important thing's life." Asked next day
what he thought of second lecture, Suzuki
said, "Excellent, but in Zen most
important thing's death." *"How can*
you say life one day and death the
next?" *"In Zen there's not much*
difference between the two." **Lois Long**
received a commission to make a design
to be printed on toilet paper.

Unstimulated by the notion of making
floral designs, she asked me if I had
any ideas. **Dollar bills.** Meals
without beans are unbeneficial.
Telephone Company should have its
system examined. Not even oriental
philosophy. Just electroanalysis. *CLV.*
He was driving a taxi in Miami to make
enough money to sit cross-legged in
Japan. *(Invitations received.* *We're*
going to the party.) California
fishermen're quarrelling with
fishermen from Equador over the right
to fish for poisoned fish. An American
lady living in Paris maintained a
bank-account in her home-town,
Buttonhole, Ohio. Finding it difficult to
keep accounts straight, she
frequently wrote to the bank asking for
extension of credit, concluding each
letter: "Love, Mrs. So-and-So." Once,
her circumstances seeming perilous,
she telegraphed. Bank replied: "Dear Mrs.
So-and-So. Don't worry. Love, Bank."
We're cheered by Berkeley, Amsterdam
(fact their city councils include

revolutionary leaders).   Nevertheless, we
know the best government's no government
at all.   We bow, not with a sense of
duty, just to save our skins.   We
renounce privileges of democracy.   We
dream of the day when no one knows who's
President, because no one bothered
to vote.   CLVI.   Hitchhiker told me all
you have to do now, no matter what city
you're in, is go to that part of town
where people are friendly.   "You don't
even have to have met them before;
they're sure to give you a place to
sleep, something to eat.   Brotherhood."
Each one of us was born by means of
an I Ching-like chance operation
(DNA-RNA; number 64, trigrams,
hexagrams.)   If life were not that
haphazard, two adults reproducing more
than once would always have the same
child.   Programmed music.   Why is it
that children, taught the names of the
months and the fact that there are twelve
of them, don't ask why the ninth is
called the seventh (September), the
tenth called the eighth (October), the
eleventh called the ninth (November), the
twelfth called the tenth (December)?
CLVII.   I was so excited when I
drove to the S&H redemption center in
Flushing that I forgot to put a dime in
the parking meter.   When I came out
with the blender and the electric
blanket I had a twenty-five-dollar ticket
on the windshield.   Sang backstage
so no one could see who it was singing.
"Who sang that song?"   What do you

want to know for?   "I want to use that
voice in my next opera."   Most people
over thirty-five're technologically
immature.   **World patriotism.**   *Ancient*
Chinese was free of syntax.   Words
floated in no-mind space.   With the
passing of centuries, fixed relations
between words became increasingly
established.   The history of Chinese
language resembles that of a human
body that, aging, becomes arthritic.
CLVIII.   Only chance to make the world a
success for humanity lies in technology,
grand possibility technology provides to do
more with less, and indiscriminately
for everyone.   Return to nature as
nature pre-technologically was,
attractive and possible as it still in
some places is, can only work for some of
us.   **After Dad died, Mother noticed I**
was filling out an application for
increasing her Social Security.   She
said, "There's something you don't
know."   I said, "Aunt Marge told me: you
were married before marrying Dad."
Mother said, "That's not all.   I was
married three times."   "What was
your first husband's name?"   Mother
said, "You know?   I've tried but
I've never been able to remember."
CLIX.   There are two kinds of music
that interest me now.   One is music I
can perform alone.   Other's music
that everyone (audience too) performs
together.   Finnegans Wake *employs syntax.*
Though Joyce's subjects, verbs and
objects are generally unconventional,

their relationships are the ordinary
ones.   Exception: the Ten Thunderclaps.
Speaking without syntax, we notice that
cadence, Dublinese or ministerial, takes
over.   (Looking out the rear-window.)
Therefore we tried whispering.

Encouraged, we began to chant.   (The
singer was sick.)   If a diabetic uses
large amounts of Vitamin C, it makes it
difficult for a doctor to analyze his
urine.   If you have gall stones and take
Vitamin C, you get worse and the gall
stones get better.   Otherwise, Vitamin C
is as close to a panacea as the human
race has managed to get.   **CLX.**
Vitamin C's one fault is that it's
cheaper and more popular than highly
advertised, often dangerous, drugs.
Therefore, the American medical-industrial
combine warns the public: Vitamin C can
be hazardous to your health.   What
they mean is: We want more of your
money.   *Asked what changes in*
Twentieth Century struck her as being
most remarkable, Margaret Mead
mentioned TV (possibility of seeing
what's happening before historians touch it
up).   **"Your thinking's full of**
holes."   That's the way I make it.
While attending an afternoon
garden-party in Paris, a French
Countess suffered an attack of
diarrhoea.   She was wearing a georgette
dress and large wide-brimmed hat.   After
some time, feeling a certain sense
of recovery, she decided to go home.   No
sooner was she in the street than she

felt her diarrhoea returning.   CLXI.
Copper essential to efficiency in our
domestic telephone system was removed
in order to establish a Vietnamese
telephone system that'd really work.
Margaret Mead mentioned hair: whether it
grows shoulder-length or longer as with
Caucasians, up and out as with Blacks, it
has proved a source of profound
irritation to the old generation.   She
said old people can't know what being
young now is like and that young people can
learn nothing from the old.   If
something won't return to nature,
return it to itself, or use it for
something otherwise useless, art, for
instance.   **Looking for some place to go,
she noticed a Metro-station.   She rushed
downstairs to the ticket-office and
asked the man there where the nearest WC
was.   He said: We don't have one.
She said: Come now, my dear man, you
must have something.   Absolutely anything
will do.**   CLXII.   Fact I was depressed
depressed him.   We don't fear anarchy:
we fear government.   *Neti-Neti:* "This
is an extremely difficult thing to
do, because it is no more an automatic
activity but depends on the strength of
our purpose to drop what has been the
framework of our lives, and see
everything afresh."   The tin and tungsten
that we're in Vietnam to get are
resources we no longer need.   While
our backs were turned, technology
changed.   USA has nothing to fight
for.   We are in Vietnam for no good

reason.   English doctor, asked what
he thought commonest human condition
was, said, "Deficient drainage."
    CLXIII.   Melody.   **He said: Well, as a
matter of fact, we do have a place, but it
doesn't seem appropriate, considering
the way you're dressed.   She said:
Lead me to it.   He took her through the
gate and half-way down the subway
platform opened a door which he
closed after she entered.**   Fuller
says words "up" and "down" are
non-descriptive of our space
existence.   We go, he says, out from or
into the earth.   Student, worried about
man's accelerated alteration of his
environment, asked where he should
look when nature's eliminated (so to
speak).   Fuller said, "Look up!"   He
could have said: Look out!   Or, even: Look
in!   CLXIV.   The motel room had ten chairs,
one of them straight-backed, two
television sets, one non-functioning,
two baths, one without hot water.   View
from the windows was of the windows in
the next building.   let Me hAve youR
baggage; i will Carry it for you.   no
nEed: i'm wearing aLl of it.   **Sometimes
we blur the distinction between art and
life; sometimes we try to clarify it.   We
don't stand on one leg.   We stand on both.**
*Lady in the Telephone Company
explained why friends, after dialing my
number, sometimes get me, sometimes get
someone else.   She said, "If someone
calls you while the circuit's overloaded,
we give'em the next number.   If your*

last digit's 3, we give'em 4.   If
circuit's still overloaded, we give'em 5,
etc.   If, after ten successive
attempts, circuit's still overloaded, we
give'em busy signal."   CLXV.   *As
population goes up, average age of
people living goes down.   Teen-agers
become the majority.   Students of
the World, Unite!   The revolution will
be simple, like rolling off a log.*   **The
outside walls of buildings in Paris are
used for transmitting ideas.   Rue de
Vaugirard, I read: La culture est
l'inversion de l'humanité.**   *The room
was very small.   The brim of her hat
touched its four walls.   There was only a
drain in the floor with two
platforms for her feet.   An automatic
flushing periodically flooded the
room.   The Metro employee returned to his
ticket-office.   To raise language's
temperature we not only remove syntax: we
give each letter undivided attention,
setting it in unique face and size;
to read becomes the verb to sing.*
CLXVI.   Day after we arrived in Los
Angeles, the police killed one
teen-ager and wounded nine others.
**Whereas getting wrong numbers used
to produce irritation among telephone
subscribers, it now brings about a sense
of community and amusement among people
otherwise unacquainted.   The New York
Telephone Company is systematically
multiplying by ten the number of each
subscriber's friends.**   *That night, while
closing up, he recalled that he had not*

noticed the lady returning through the
gate.   He decided to check whether
or not she was still in the station.   As
he came down the platform toward the
WC, he heard loud beating on the
door and her shouts from within.

CLXVII.   Once France got out of
Vietnam, Paris filled up with excellent
Vietnamese restaurants.   Vietnamese food
should be made generally available in
New York and Washington.   Though less
pleasant efforts have failed, a few good
meals might end the war.   A new society
exists with its own supplies and
demands.   A musician now makes his way in
the world without waiting to be fifty
years old.   Not so long ago, sources
of money were so thoroughly cut off that
most gifted musicians gave up before
they were thirty just in order to eat.

After he opened the door, she
furiously complained that he had
locked her in.   Denying this and
wishing to demonstrate how she herself
might have opened the door from the
inside, he took her back with him into
the closet and closed the door.

CLXVIII.   Been robbed so often he's
losing his sense of property.   **All**
efforts of the two of them failed.   The
door remained shut.   They spent the night
together.   The room was flushed every few
minutes.   The Countess's dress was
drenched.   The workman's face became
seriously irritated by the brim of the
Countess's hat which remained on.   Her

diarrhoea continued.   <u>Lots of
mimeographed material's placed everyday
in the faculty mail slots at the School
of Music.</u>   Manuscript exhibitions are
held in the hall outside.   The
<u>largest exhibition in history was given
by one of the instructors.</u>   Instead of
<u>throwing his year's mail away unread as
the other faculty members had, he had
saved every scrap.</u>   CLXIX.   "We'll be
remembered as those who lived in the
age of Buckminster Fuller."   After
Fuller's third lecture at Town Hall,
capacity audience gave him standing
ovation.   Commenting on this, Fuller
said, "It wasn't for me; I'm only an
average man.   It was for what I'd been
saying: the fact it's possible to
make life a success for everyone."   In
and out.   **We're taking first steps.
Soon we'll be able to walk.**   Preach.
We practice what we practice.   *As we
were walking along, she smiled and
said, "You're never bored, are you."
(Boredom dropped when we dropped our
interest in climaxes.*   Socrate.   *Even
at midnight we can tell the difference
between two Chinamen.   Grey's
differentiated.   Johns.   Traffic's
never twice the same.   We stay awake
and listen or we go to sleep and dream.)*
     **CLXX.   It used to be beautiful.   Was
like a park.   Now it's like a parking lot.**
Another wealthy American woman living
in Paris gave a dinner party.   For the
entertainment of her guests she had
engaged a string quartet.   After their

performance, she gave the first
violinist an envelope, saying, "Here's
something that may enable you to
enlarge your little orchestra."   Satie:
     "We must be uncompromising to the end."
Do nothing for one reason only.   Think
it with respect to a large number of
other reasons, preferably reasons
that're seemingly contradictory.   **After**
hearing the end of the story, he said,
     "That doesn't seem to be the end."   Of
     course, he's right.   The story goes on
and on.   CLXXI.   The young are
technologically grown-up.   (Music's
definitely improving.   You can tell it
     from the fact that more and more you
hear it in places where you can move
around.   You don't sit in rows facing the
stage.   It's no longer disturbing to
yourself or others if during the
performance you get up and leave.)   Edwin
Schlossberg told me that while Fuller
was writing a dedication in his book
     Utopia or Oblivion, he paused and
said, "Those are not the only
     possibilities."   American government.
Its head is in the clouds: it takes the
government of other countries more
seriously than it does its own.   CLXXII.
     We no longer have servants.   We have
hostesses.   The black one is even more
     charming than the white one.   **She**
said she couldn't take a large,
comprehensive view of life because of
     the painfulness of immediate events
     in the lives of her children.   She
     needs to become blind in order to see

through and beyond.   (Necessary pain.)
Technoanarchism (Kostelanetz).   After
the operation, she complained of a new
and unusual ache.   Doctor said: It
must be in your head.   However, X-rays
showed he had forgotten to take his
scissors out when he sewed her up.   The
reason we like black people isn't
because they're black.   We like them
because they're not as grey as we are.
        **CLXXIII.   Picnic preparation in hotel
room.   Chicken, marinated in lemon and
sake, wrapped'n'foil, left overnight,
next day dipped in sesame oil and
charcoal-broiled.   Broccoli, sliced, was
put with ginger in twenty-five packages;
corn, still in husks, silk removed,
buttered'n'wrapped.   Noticing bathtub was
full of salad, he said, "I don't want
any hairs in my food."**   When can we
get together?   "It's hard to say: I'm
going out of town tomorrow and I'll be
back sometime today."   Stopped at a gas
station around noon, the second week of
May, in a part of Ohio I had heard
was excellent for finding morels.   I
asked the attendant if he would direct me
to a woods where I could hunt.
Looking at his wrist watch, he said, "It's
too late."   CLXXIV.   "Do you have a
good heart?"   I enjoy doing what I do.
And I am glad to be with you.   **Fame has
advantages.   Anything you do gets used.**
        Society places no obstacles.   **Also**
you become of some help to those who
aren't famous yet.   Activity.   "What's
your favorite color?"   I didn't

answer.   "What's your favorite combination
of colors?"   Didn't answer.   When he
was in Art School, he told me, no one
liked orange and red together.   Then a
teacher came to the school who loved
orange and red together.   All the
students changed their minds.   They
discovered that they all loved
orange and red together.   **CLXXV.   Times
published a news release from the Food
and Drug Administration listing
marketed drugs that were hazardous or
ineffectual.   There was then an
unexpected run on the market.
Customers apparently feared that their
favorite remedies would become
unavailable.   Settling down for the
night, Thoreau's Indian guide said,
"There are snakes here."   Thoreau
said, "Snakes don't bother me."   Indian
said they didn't bother him either.**
Debug world program for any
kind'o'living.   (We are in our technological
infancy.   [Tesla, who discovered
alternating current, did so in this
century.]   Technological errors made
by government, industry [DDT, ABM, SST,
CIA, etc.] are those of children, who,
even though they don't know what the
score is, go on playing
pre-technological games of power and
profit.)   CLXXVI.   *Our Spring Will
Come.*   That was the title of Pearl
Primus's dance for which I wrote music in
the 'forties.   It will,—of course
Spring will come.   But before it does no
amount of good weather keeps us from

thinking we're in for a few more

storms.　　　We no longer need to dig in

the earth for mercury.　　　We have it in

our oceans.　　　"All we have to do is

collect it when it's washed up on

the beaches": Edwin Schlossberg.　　　**Susan**

spent three years in Europe, then

was obliged to return to the US.　　　She

told me she was surprised to find things

were going on more or less as usual.　　　She

had expected to find herself in the

midst of violence, destruction,

revolution.　　　*CLXXVII.　　　Church was bombed.*

Façade remains.　　　Two men came to an

intersection.　　　One was blind and

accompanied by his seeing-eye dog.

While they waited for the light to

change, dog pissed on his master's leg.

Blind man then fed dog some beef.　　　Other

man said: Why reward'im?　　　(Pissed on

your leg.)　　　"I'm not rewarding'im.　　　I'm

finding out where his head is so I can

kick him in the ass."　　　Paper should be

edible, nutritious.　　　Inks used for

printing or writing should have

delicious flavors.　　　Magazines or

newspapers read at breakfast should be

eaten for lunch.　　　Instead of throwing

one's mail in the waste-basket, it

should be saved for the dinner guests.

CLXXVIII.　　　Young man came to my office in

the university.　　　I asked, "What class are

you in?"　　　He said he wasn't in any

class.　　　He studied whatever he wanted

to without being enrolled.　　　That way

he'd gone to several universities,

leaving each when there was no further

class he found useful to attend.   He
said, "I'm about to graduate from this
place."   Nanette Hassell's dream: The
adopted children wore hats that made
them look like mushrooms.   One of them
explained why they were all so hungry:
"Sometimes when he's working he
forgets to feed us."   **Pittsburgh steel
companies now know how to keep from
polluting air and water.   But it'd cost
too much money, they say; they say they
wouldn't have any left to pay
employees.   When they see how rich
Fuller's Pollution Exploitation Corporation
gets, they'll change their minds and
claim that, after all, all that stuff is
really theirs.**

MUSHROOM BOOK

I

Bake *Polyporus frondosus* (buttered,
seasoned, covered)
until tender. Chop.
Steep wild rice 5 x 20′
in boiling water (last water salted).
Combine.

Voices singing Joyce's Ten Thunderclaps
transformed
electronically to fill actual
thunder envelopes; strings playing star
maps transformed likewise to fill
actual raindrop envelopes (rain
falling on materials representing history of
technology).
(McLuhan.) Last rain not falling
(wind instruments), i.e. present moment.
Music becomes nature (Johns).

Man/Earth: a problem to be
solved.

highway system (Ivan Illich): a false utility.

no water unless necessary.

Hunting for *hygrophoroides*, found
abortivus instead.
Returning to get more *abortivus*, found
ostreatus in fair condition. South to
see the birds, spotted *mellea*.
Hunting is starting from
zero, not looking for.

Boletus.

Went to meet Peggy at the airport.
Found myself in Japanese crowd
(popular politician arriving in the same plane
from Europe). Jet with engines going drove
near to us. (Rare opportunity.) Was
surprised to see people putting fingers in
their ears.

Stew *oreades* in beer and
butter.

September to November.

9. *Suillus
granulatus.*
Under white pine
more frequently
than any other,
late summer and
fall.

10. *Suillus
albidipes.*
Under pine,
often in
plantations of
white pine, late
summer and fall.

11. *Suillus
brevipes.* Late
summer and fall
under 2 or 3
needle pines.

12. *Gyroporus
cyanescens.*
Edible and

choice (if you
can effectively
remove the
sand), summer
and fall,
especially along
roadsides or
beside trails.
(Alexander H. Smith
and Harry D. Thiers)

what was her naMe
(she lived in the countrY)?
she Couldn't
dEcide
whether or Not
the mushroom wAs edible. she

telePhoned to say:
don't eat it, it may be poisonoUs.
motheR replied:
don't be foolish, it wAs delicious.

We know when we hear the motorcycles
we're on the other
side of the mountain. We then go to the
place where *craterellus* grows. Easy there
to find the path that leads to the
trailer-camp.

There's no alternative to Fuller's realization:
As long as one human being's
hungry, the entire race is hungry. Human
nature changes spiritually when
material needs're met.

Tube trama of the *Xerocomus*
subtype (weakly divergent), the hyphae
tubular.
(Alexander H. Smith and Harry D. Thiers)

He intuitively knew that the
truth (not whispered)
was to be given to the youth apolitically.
Only hope? "A good
one."

I can remove the bitterness, he said.
Onion in butter, then the
naucinoides cut in pieces, stems chopped.
He added pepper, lemon, caraway
seed. No salt.
It was delicious. He said that dill could
have been used instead of the seeds.

we find iT
in the haveRstraw cemetery
ordInarily
in oCtober;
but tHis
October
not onLy
have i nOt found one
but other Mushrooms
generAlly there are also rare.

i noticed, i thought, a *Pholiota* (*autumnalis?*);
also a fEw
dwaRfed
naucinoideS;
nO puff balls,
No
Agaricus.
noThing,
not even the Usual
Marasmius.

. . . that this poisonous species and
some edible ones cannot be distinguished
from each other at this
stage except by studying the cuticle of
each button under the
microscope.
(Alexander H. Smith)

Is it or was it too late?
(Apocalypse.) Gunther Stent said
human brain worked up
until 1850.

Matters have been arranged so
that it will come about with or without him.
(He arranged them that way.) We are already
accustomed to the fact that he is nowhere
to be seen, "he passeth by—".

Fear, clarity, power, old age:
obstacles one removes with
invention.

Moving around, we take concerts and exhibitions
with us. There is no
connected administration. We are audience
and visitors. There are no special hours or
places. We also manage in
spite of all the entertainment to
get some work done.

great fungi, six.
(Henry David Thoreau)

Not only the foliage begins to look
dark and dense, but many ferns are fully
grown. (Henry David Thoreau)

Martino told me reason his lamb chops're better
than Ottomanelli's was his business's
smaller. Margaret Mead,
too, insisted on importance
of less numbers (if one's a futurist).

ing and yellowing the grass, as if a
liquor (or dust) distilled from them.
(Henry David Thoreau)

Holding her knife in
her right hand,
lady-psychoanalyst rushed to reach the
mushroom first. When she saw her left
hand getting near, not hesitating, she cut
herself.

Who's been killed
by a work of art?

Brown's letter: Ellul says human nature has
been destroyed, that

food must become entirely artificial.
There is no hope in
counter-culture ("nothing there to build
on"). Brown made me read Ellul.

II

We're in a confusion of
books. Bonfire?

Sandwiches of leftover
mushrooms.

Plan (which Grace agrees
to): to visit the school in Baltimore,
one, two, three,
four or five days after the first
November rain.
That way I'll get to revisit
Bombay Hook (peak of
Canadian geese) and the woods
near Smyrna (excellent for
fungi).

We have turned
around: We live in another direction.

Work's a series of replies
without regrets.

Cantharellus chocolate
Clitocybe Amanita Tubes
Neurophyllum Stirps Michigan Never List Plate
Miscellaneous Plate Before
The not Precautions *Pholiota lissia*
Edible *Amanita* Cooke

elongate *Harpochytrium* The
The Several
honey-yellow *Hygrophorus Di-mon* The *Agaricus*
Helvella.

often.

S.wideantsfindpresomebeandmon
backocnorflocthetertoa
G.brownca
OFchestpudevisuningquentlysubin
fersnamenutenasbeechcoineachitsnotofclosand
B.
TIring.

When I mentioned the three factors given by
Ellul that "could
change the course of
history" (general war with
enormous destruction; upsetting the
technological world on the part of an increasing
number of people; intervention
on the part of a decided God), he
said, "The third is the most
likely."

Looked up invention in telephone book:
Inventaprises Inc
Inventive Design Inc
Inventive Music Ltd
Invento Prods Corp.

We remain greedy: we never find
enough. We keep on
looking for mushrooms

until we're obliged (an engagement or the fact
the light's failing) to stop. Only for
some such reason do we leave the woods (unless,
by then, we're lost).

We imagine that
spores that never before joined in
reproduction on occasion in the case of
related species sometimes do:
possibility of a
natural invention.

What is that now
ancient and decayed
fungus by the first
mayflowers, —trumpet-shaped with a
very broad mouth, the chief
inner part green, the outer dark brown?
. . . dirty-white fungi in nests. Each one is
burst a little at the
top, and is full of dust
of a yellowish rotten-stone
color, which is perfectly dry.
(Henry David Thoreau)

voroisbnybnaetn
egcotooev
IAschmK.

Go to work, and above all co-operate
and don't hold back.
(R. Buckminster Fuller)

Hunting on pkway: civil
disobedience.

In woods, we're misled
by leaves or play of
sunlight; driving along, we sometimes
stop, park, and get
out, only to discover it's a football or a
piece of trash. Learning from such
experiences isn't what we do.

matsutake. L. rachodes. umbonatus.
(Map showing locations)

sInuUsrrn.snnenhL.hmecusoaenilsiw
aWhhdm.

Tendency to
counteract: hunting in the same places.

Music ("good
music") excludes the stranger, establishes the
government, renders
the composer deaf. Is't because connection of
state'n'art was
clearer to them than others that
Chinese (twice at
least)'ve shaken'em apart?

Mosquitoes that bite us while we're
finding mushrooms
don't bother us.

E. (from *Solo for Voice 79*)

trgOn efosnr uJvaR mbthr
mnols htbu.

back on one another
or try to gain at the expense

of another. Any success in such lopsidedness
will be increasingly
short-lived.
(R. Buckminster Fuller)

In 1935 when I first
arrived in Huautla in quest of
the sacred mushrooms no one
would speak to me about them.
(R. Gordon Wasson)

Eat only small portions, . . . half a head
the first time. Be sure
each member of the family follows the same
procedure. It does not follow that because
father can eat them mother and all the
children can do likewise.
(Alexander H. Smith)

III

"The situation is
changing rapidly. Don't read Ellul. Read *The
Chinese Road to Socialism*
(Wheelwright and McFarlane). Fight
self[1] (Self-Interest).
Serve the People.[2] I.e. Fight Profit motive,[3]
consumer economy, technique in command.[4]
Choose Redness over
Expertness."
1. Duchamp and Zen.
2. Buckminster Fuller. 3. Thoreau.
4. Anarchy.

tala.

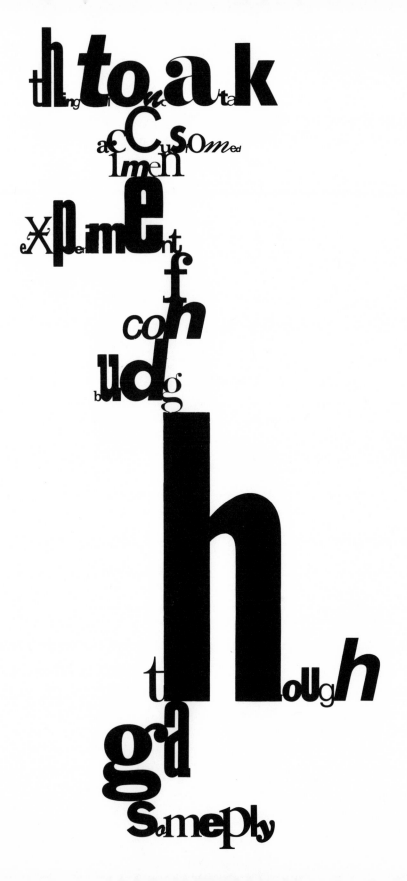

In the early 'thirties Cowell
introduced me to oriental
musics. I was
attracted by the
rhythmic structure and rhythmic
complexity of North
Indian music.

No mushrooms in the woods? Let's go
buy some real ones.

During the
transit strike in
New York City many people became
hitchhikers. I
picked up a South
American. We got into a
conversation. He turned out to be a composer
whose principal hobby was hunting
wild mushrooms.

It is neither long nor short, big
nor small, but transcends
all limits, . . . and
every method of
treating it concretely. It is
the substance you see
before you—begin to reason
about it and you at once fall
into error.
(Hsi Yun recorded by P'ei Hsiu)

4 notes. (*Cheap Imitation*, sketch, II:
XXXI)

IV

larpahas-conthe.

Eat together.

in key than wet is
    the little skørhat fall.
    Clitocybe examination
      with *Cocos* hyphae or
      There
      of and laevigatum down
        down depressed

on "Sacred

        made are asema Macrae
     ascus Great
        proved Coast the
  prolate then have buff.

tempo of Korean classical music.

     senadseenetsgttipinnsmfe
    nhnhdspntfeBrshnchhniaoionppn
     lurpeeane.

To finish for Lois programmed
        handwritten mushroom
book
including mushroom stories,
excerpts from (mushroom) books,
remarks about (mushroom) hunting,
excerpts from Thoreau's *Journal*
   (fungi),
excerpts from Thoreau's *Journal*
     (entire),

remarks about:
Life/Art,
Art/Life,
Life/Life,
Art/Art,
Zen,
Current reading,
Cooking (shopping, recipes),
Games, Music mss., Maps,
Friends,
Invention,
Projects,
+
Writing without syntax,
Mesostics (on mushroom names).

Polyporus frondosus. (Map showing
location)

We only need boots, basket, paper bags,
and knife.

head are work
and, it caps. Huautla
base species along
diam; Mounce *Amanita*
beautiful be coniferous edible
clavipes view of
drying ("snuff-brown")
germinated to to an
hues
an
Gylden Sabina fungi. From Huautla,
the taette. body
gills
reason of
August

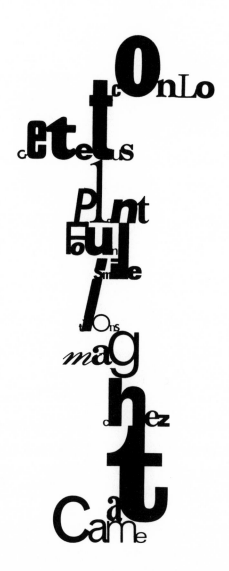

experimentation, free to branches projections
(White
size. all
cups. of in the
and Agaric.

Guy Nearing told
us it's a good idea when hunting
mushrooms to have a pleasant goal, a
waterfall for instance, and, having reached
it, to return
another way. When, however, we're obliged
to go and come back by the same path,
returning we notice
mushrooms we hadn't noticed going out.

Armillaria mellea: Roast
without seasoning on bed
of salt.

Music willy-nilly.

Dad's oil
dehydrator was a contained
electrostatic field, one electrode down the
center, the other
the container's inner wall.
Principal problem was finding a
dielectric to separate the two. Refuse oil
poured in came out as oil of highest grade,
dry chemicals, and drinking water.
Petroleum Rectifying Company
successfully prohibited
its use.

the sands of the Ganges.
(Hsi Yun recorded by
P'ei Hsiu)

My mushroom books and pamphlets
(over three hundred items)
will go soon to Chadwick (gardener who
knows how to hunt and who is
surrounded by youth
he's inspired).
"You must meet our wizard,"
Nobby said.

Using *I Ching* we found
four places in
Manhattan to go and listen: excellent way to
spend your time if you
have nothing better to do.

AOAsclt.

V

he Suddenly said,
"sTop!"
gReat
quantities Of it were growing near the
road.
his name was fletcher Pence.
after Hurried
exAmination i decided it was
pRobably
an *agarIcus*. we filled
bAgs and baskets.

guy neaRing had never seen it
before.
"it mUst be
a new *aGaricus!*" i decided
tO take it to town and
Serve it
tO friends

At a party.
fortuNately
No one the next day was
ill. lois took
specimens
to
ann arbor.
dr.
smith immediately took
down

icones
farlowianae
and opened
it to *stropharia rUgoso*. we had proven its
edibiLity, though we did so
foolishly.
As he asked,
we senT him (to his surprise)
A bushel of dried material.

nytrinattaua.

Usually we hunt with our stomachs, disdaining
fungi we don't know to be edible. As a science,
botany's a newcomer.
(Perhaps because most always did
and do as we.) New York State wasn't
lavish in its support of Peck's
research, nor was Farlow
without hesitation made
a member of the Harvard
faculty.

Hypomyces lactifluorum. (Map showing
location)

Morels?
(Wristwatch.)
"T's too late."

I have a sneaking
hankering to go again to Arcata
Bottom (Hortense
Lanphere's land between the ocean and the
lagoon) soon: late this month or
early December. We'll find
the *matsutake* (tastes
like pine). It travels
well: I'll fill the freezer (she
doesn't like them). I'll
stay with Morris in the house in
the woods by the lake.

skørhat any are wall *Entolomes*
cap in specimens. layer
mito-
chondria Little *Russula*
vaccinum Plane
grows (Black pores less plants structural non
for-
ests *particulier gennemskaret* we subhymenium
illustrated, the basidia
It to of other *corralloides* a at
Hydnum son crude Dept.
nucleus has peyote
elle
Although *bien*.

Fuller: Don't change Man; change
his environment. Mao: Remould
people to their very souls;
revolutionize
their thinking. (Find
common denominator.)

And I was attracted by the
natural noises of
breathing in Japanese shakuhachi
playing. However, instead
of studying with
an oriental master, I chose to study
with Arnold
Schoenberg.

raisedul.

When we find mushrooms in
perfect condition, we have a
musical delight (not that
arising from being on the beat:
just the pleasure of coincidence).

cAesar's
Mushroom:
we hAd them first
iN vermont.
they were gIven
To us
by A stranger.

they were even more deliCious when
with jAp
wE found them
at ediSto.
he sAutéed them
veRy
gEntly
And, at the last
moment,
added whipped cream.

lost landmarks.

Poisonous Fungi. (Charles H. Peck)

Find the haircapped moss in November and in
it you'll find *umbonatus*,
the grey chanterelle.

Everett Reimer's
*Essay on Alternatives in
Education* begins with a quotation from
Margaret Mead: "My
grandmother wanted me to
have an education, so she kept
me out of school."
Reimer works with Illich in Cuernavaca.

Those which are ripe
are so softened at the top
as to admit the rain
through the
skin . . . , and the interior is shaking like
a jelly, and if you open it
you see what looks like a yellowish gum.
(Henry David Thoreau)

He (Arnold
Schoenberg) impressed upon me
the need for a musical
structure (the division of a
whole into parts);
he believed this should be brought about
through pitch relations. But since I was
working with noises, . . .

Whuzat? "Just another ugly
sound."

Freedom from likes and
dislikes, the sudden sense of
identification, the spirit
of comedy. Morris said that some time after
we'd left, they got
to talking. "The
difference between you and them is they're
looking for solutions; you don't
think there're any
problems."

VI

We played chess together.
Why had he thought
I was a good
player?

It's like an Easter egg hunt. "Eggs that no one
has hidden."

cecaslistunamo
the
wumoatrunac
ralenet
hreness
igo
irntsprilld.
Plant is of them,
sound.
with small from the
young
Cap is sometimes marked to cases
the thin young and two species.

We study . . . forms . . .
(Henry David Thoreau)

You can tell if you're
in an attractive American spot: it's
littered with trash.

the frenCh call it
tRompette des morts. its
colors

blAck
To
grEy
woRk
to hidE it, but not
effectiveLy (we overcome
aLl
sUch
natural deviceS).

deviCes, natural but
undergrOund, inexplicable,
some yeaRs keep it from
appeariNg: we looked this year
for
instance
'till we were blUe
in the faCe
withOut success. another year
all you had to do was
Park,
go In
any wOods:
there were mIllions of them
everywhere.
they Dry
wEll
for winter uSe.

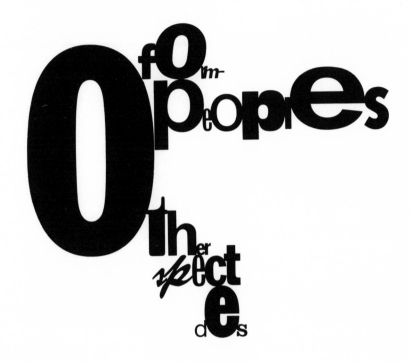

Of Other People's Form-Expected Odds

What's brewing in China?
                (November 7 issue
of *Observer*)

we're tiCkled pink
        At the thought
    of fiNding
    black Trumpets
        tHe
        sAme day we find the little
  cinnabaR
        onEs.
    the
    two coLors
            Linked
        fUlfill
 one
   among
our many Summer desires.

        Cooked together,
     they
make a
     beautIful dish.
        aNd their flavors, like their colors,
complemeNt
     one Another.
     when
fall
  comes
  we're oBliged
    to chAnge
      ouR
       desIres.
        oNe of them we have then is to find on
            the same day

the
lilac
personatUm and
the
buff-
colored
oreadeS; we then broil the former having
stuffed
its caps
with the latter.

It's when I know what to do that it's
boring.

ivinesslylieua
augatiutarxoted
imaninn
optar
roidulstempsfe.

(noises), the pitch
relations of which were
not defined, I
needed another basis for musical
structure. This I found in
sound's duration parameter,
sound's only
parameter which is present even when
no sound is intended.

We're instructed by nature. There's no
natural boundary, Indira Gandhi said, when they
asked why she
didn't close it.
People come and go quite freely. In removing
boundaries is the
preservation of the World.

We're no longer satisfied by going to
the lecture: we want to have the
experience itself.

Her doctoral thesis was the study of
one square foot of land.
She named all the plants
she found on it. Undoubtedly
we learn (though we don't know what) by
returning each year to the
same places. Our circumstances are
changing, however; now we're here
and now we're
there (Minnesota;
Minnesota).

They impress me like humors . . . pimples on the face
of the earth, . . . A sort of excrement they
are.   (Henry David Thoreau)

i sPent
twO years in
iLlinois (the state
is
almost
totallY cultivated: there are
few Places in which
tO hunt). i found
veRy few mushrooms
Until i met
joe kaStelic and bill stank.

Finally, bill and joe
took me Reluctantly
tO a farm
west

of
   champaigN.
      they tolD me that
         if i tOld
   anyone elSe
       aboUt the place
     that
  they
would cut
   my ballS off.

           i Had collected enough to feed that
                    percentage
        of
     100
     people
   who would
      willinglY eat it.
   reichert anD shaller
      had fouNd me that morning at the edge of
                  the lake.
they
gave me the blUe-jean jacket
  (st. ives deniM)

     that
  i'm now weaRing. lost in
      muskEg
      i had sPent the night
        Asleep
        oN a squirrel's
        miDden. my food had been
 a
roast of *boletUs:* it was juicier than
  the *repanduM.*

VII

They continue as is. "Changing'd cost
too much."

Asked Arragon, the
historian, about history.
He said you have to invent it.

Aug. 11. P.M.—To Assabet
Bath.
I have heard since the 1st of
this month the steady creaking cricket.
Some are digging
early potatoes. I notice a new growth of red
maple sprouts, small
reddish leaves surmounting light-green
ones, the old being
dark-green. Green lice on
birches.   (Henry David
Thoreau)

He was silent for
two years, and then he spoke the truth.

A crescent of light.
(Henry David Thoreau)

Since Dad invented at home, he was kept busy
running errands for
Mother.

Jasper Johns.

Pileus clavate,
often irregular or compressed and
somewhat lobed, obtuse, glabrous,

yellow, tapering below
into the short, rather distinct, yellowish or
whitish stem, spores narrowly
elliptical, .0003 to
.0004 inch long.
. . . closely resembles the typical European
plant, but usually the
clubs or caps are
curved, twisted,
compressed or lobed in such a way, that it
is difficult to find two plants just alike.
(Charles H. Peck)

I made what I called macromicrocosmic rhythmic
structures characterized by a whole
having that number of
units that each unit had of measures.

We converse as we hunt as
though we are in a living room.

Pileus 6-10 cm
broad, convex to broadly convex or
finally nearly plane; surface
dry and matted-fibrillose, becoming more
conspicuously fibrillose in
age, . . . becoming duller . . .
(Alexander H. Smith and Harry D. Thiers)

matsutake ya   mushroom
shiranu ko no ha no   ignorance leaf of tree
hebaritsuku   adhesiveness
(Bashō)
After say eight years I made my
translation: What mushroom?
What leaf?

ioioieneaprooeearnd.

the Chinese are hoping to
prevent the contamination of the
environment—pollution . . . —*before* it
becomes (as . . . in our industrialised West) a
major, almost
insurmountable disaster.
(Felix Greene)

To mushroom mushroom have become
from

have the top

details for

the fruiting important
or special
mushrooms. Hard summer

key should be

true to important morel

to the

different it. Field are same
characteristic.

I had unintentionally infuriated
a community of
yellow-jackets by stepping on their home.
They attacked. Forgetting my love of mushrooms
and the pleasure of being in the
woods, I took off my shirt to use as a
weapon against them.
Thirty-five stung. These stings,
friends said, were medicine for
my arthritis.

in July.   (Henry David Thoreau)

To remove the rubbery
quality of chanterelles slice them
thinly. Cook them
quickly (not long and
slowly as some advise) in butter
and a little olive oil
with some salt
(preferably Kosher salt). Towards the
end, add La Victoria taco sauce
generously. This
sauce brings out the mushroom's peppery
quality which
otherwise has a tendency to
disappear.

like the void, in which there is
no confusion or evil. (Hsi Yun recorded by
P'ei Hsiu)

Ellul's book's a work of art: it has only one
idea. It could use som'others.

This structure resembles
Indian tala but
it depends on
ending.

those who seek the goal through intellection
are like the fur
(many) and those who
obtain intuitive knowledge of the Way like the
horns (few).   (Hsi Yun recorded by
P'ei Hsiu)

Hygrophorus penarius.
Nomi dialettali romagnoli: Nessuno.
(Pietro Zangheri)

eerat? ogooeonemthwaroweton

emomo blarcaw uttol

lomct

We brought such a great variety of mushrooms
from Vermont to the Four Seasons, the cook
was confused. They fired

us.

We play games in the
evening (backgammon, sometimes
chess) and, when it's possible,
chess the late
afternoon. On
vacation, after breakfast, we play
all day: chess, backgammon,
dominoes. At Nag's Head (the
Bensons') I won a
backgammon
tournament (have
certificate to prove it).

For jewels they have no longing and
for stinking filth they have no loathing.

(Hsi Yun recorded
by P'ei Hsiu)

For the most part, we just
use butter, salt and pepper,
and let it go at that (we want to taste the
mushroom). Joe Hyde,
however, says that there isn't anything
that isn't improved by a little lemon
juice. Sometimes I go overboard:
dip seaweed in soy
sauce and wasabi and wrap it around broiled
stuffed mushroom caps.

We like our friends the way
they are. The closest ones take
liberties, invite
themselves to dinner.

to-day. (Henry David Thoreau)

ahachudegnathe e
lubuta
ne

VIII

Eddie Schlossberg told me of
the seven or eight
young people who changed the structure of the
mental hospital in Galesburg,
simply taking as premise the
fact that the
inmates were not insane. *"Faites quelque chose."*

Besides mushrooms, Nearing introduced me to the
catbrier (good for salad) and the
fragrant goldenrod (good for
tea).

It depends on beginning and ending (it's an
object, whereas tala facilitates the process of
improvisation.

I was surprised in the open markets in
Finland to see poisonous mushrooms for
sale (poisonous, that is, according to French
and American authors). Finns cook
chanterelles as though they too are
poisonous.

Sept. 2. For three weeks the woods have
　　　　had a strong musty smell
　　　from decaying fungi. The
　　maple-leaved viburnum berries
　　　　are a dark purple or black
　　now. They are scarce. The red
　　　pyrus berries are ripe. The
　　dense oval bunches of arum
berries now startle the walker in swamps.
　　　　(Henry David Thoreau)

　　　　I've finished "studying
being interrupted": prefer it to not.

　　Comatus: wine and parmesan.

We drove off the parkway and parked, then walked
　　　　　　back to the bushes
　　　　　of blackberries we
　　　　had noticed. We did this
　　　　hoping to avoid being
stopped by policemen. Nevertheless, one of them
　　　　　shortly was yelling:
Get out! No blackberry picking! As we were
　　　leaving, we luckily found a culvert
　　　in which, hidden, we each picked
five quarts.

　　look.

　　　　　taversultiontaoftabty
raofsuchknownofthe
roomthislivewillythis
　　thetheersuchtheattheedfieldsa
　　pladocishcoed.

We are friends a long time.

      this speCies
          Looks
            lIke *armillaria mellea*
        buT
      it has nO ring. i found it this year
      in montClair
    in quantitY: i filled
      seven Bags and could
        havE filled more.

        iT is one of my
        fAvorites.
    something aBout
        its tExture, particularly the
        texture
    of the Stalks,
    slightly Crisp,
      is vEry
      pleasiNg.
a little lemon helpS its taste.

        U.S. is losing
      financial power. That
          alone'll improve
    our credit.

I can do many things at once: stand in line,
  listen to the music, have ideas, wait for the
    next conversation. Besides having
    ideas, I compose them in *I Ching* given
numbers of words, letters or syllables.

      universal mind is no mind . . . and
        is completely detached from
  form.   (Hsi Yun recorded by P'ei Hsiu)

Asked Hyde how to cook garlic sausage I'd bought.
Hyde: Study it.

Hydneae. Hedgehog
Mushrooms. In the family *Hydneae*, the cap,
when present, has neither gills nor pores on its
lower surface, but
instead of these there are
numerous spine-like or
awl-shaped teeth.
(Charles H. Peck)

Game remains unfinished. Which of us'll win?

Frie   „Sporebillede"
Tilheftede   (Faelninger af
Udrandede   sporer.
Fastvoksede
Nedløbende
Nedløbende med tand
Savtakkede
Forskellige Typer af Lameller
(Else and Hans Hvass)

IX

in Connecticut
in the lAte
afterNoon, nobby and i
frequenTly
went to tHe woods.
he'd hike Ahead
Rapidly
(to gEt exercise, i
suppose).

i waLked
sLowly
not wanting any fUngi
to eScape my notice.

on sUndays
soMetimes
Beth, becky and suki
wOuld
come aloNg with us.
eAch
Then (nobby too)
had
a bag or a basket. on sUch
family occaSions, nobby covered no
more
ground than
the rest of
us.

A-ki. (from *Solo for Voice
60*)

react against complex
structures and
heaviness.
(E. L. Wheelwright and Bruce McFarlane)

However, I came to no
longer feel the need for
musical structure. Its absence could,
in fact, blur the
distinction between art
and life. An individual can hear sounds
as music (enjoy living) whether or not he is at a
concert.

having this experience
today, one has it as Daniel did in
the Lion's Den. Many forces, competitive
self-interest and devotion to efficiency
among them, have brought mankind and the earth
itself to the edge of
oblivion.

Three species are included here. They all lack
a ring on the stalk . . . though a veil is
present . . .

KEY TO SPECIES

1. Cap brick-red; common on oak
   logs and stumps, usually until late
   in the fall . . . .
   . . . . . *Naematoloma sublateritium*
1. Color of cap orange cinnamon to
   yellow or olive 2
2. Cap orange-cinnamon to tawny
   . . . . *Naematoloma capnoides*
2. Cap and gills yellow becoming
   olivaceous . . . .
   . . . . *Naematoloma fasciculare*

(Alexander H. Smith)

Quelet asserts
that it is better raw than cooked
and that its sweet milk affords an agreeable drink
for the botanist in the warm
days of summer.

(Charles H. Peck)

2

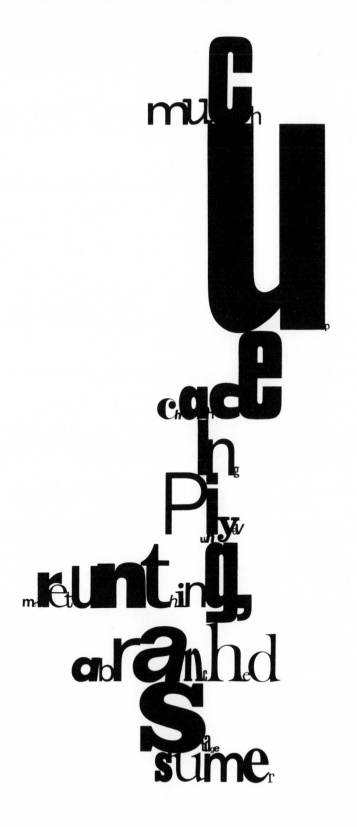

Make a book that's edible.

. . . the earth itself to the edge of
oblivion. Total destruction can be
                        averted and a change for
                        the good of all men
                        may be made, but it
will require selfless intelligence
and cooperative energetic work.

Flore
alynatiqUe
champigNons
ouvraGe
prIx.

As we were leaving the airport
                Morris said: First
            thing's to take a ride on the lake. I
said, "What for? Mushrooms don't grow on
lakes." Years later, Ted's voice came over
            the water: Mushrooms! Rowing out,
filled canoe with *pleuroti.*

üMarmürkel
sOögiseen
kübaR
Cm.
kollakasHall
tumEdamate
heLedamate
aLumises
servAs

Eraldatud
jalaSt
Cm,
värvusetUd,
toLvjalt
tippudEga,
rohtuNud
aprillisT
mAini.

Since *Tarzetta* is the oldest of
these three generic
names, the choice of one of these
species as the lectotype of
Tarzetta would lead to
the abandonment of either *Stromantinia* or
Geopyxis, both
widely used generic names.
This led Rifai (1968) to propose the
conservation of *Geopyxis* over
Tarzetta, and to
Dumont and Korf's decision to accept
Tarzetta over
Stromantinia. (*Mycologia LXIII:*
1084, 1971)

shelf-shape.
(Henry David Thoreau)

lost.

When we first moved to the
country we were seven friends: Paul and Vera,
David and M.C., Karen and
David Weinrib and I. Paul and Vera stayed in
Garnerville while houses were being built. The
rest of us lived in the farmhouse

on the land. After
seventeen years only David Tudor and
Karen remain. All the
couples have split up.

Tihti
seRvaga
peenvIltja
Cm.
eosleHekesed
vOi
vaLkjasbeezikad
hOredalt
Monikord
nogusAlt

kunI
eRaldatavad.
valkjasbeezIkas
kollakaspruuNikas,
kUiv
cM.

"becauSe
of iTs
shaggy appeaRance
and dull cOlor
it has Been
nIcknamed
the oLd man
Of the woods."
its new naMe,
academicallY speaking,
is *floCcopus.*
guy nEaring
doeSn't accept the new name.

loiS and I
disagree abouT
its desiRability
as fOod. she likes it
Because
"It
Looks like
A prune but tastes like
a Clod
of Earth."   sari also likes
it
very mUch.
She makes a pickle out of
it.

X

(4) "In the end, even law disappears"
p. 298. A consummation devoutly to be wished
by all good Christians, Nietzscheans and
Marxists.
(5) Police terror disappears, p. 413.
And police disappear, p. 297: "a
progressive emptying of legal forms and a
consequent gain in
human techniques which render a gendarmery
useless."
(6) Beyond Good and Evil: . . . Hurrah!
(Norman O. Brown)

Last year, the
last three weeks of
August, the woods were
filled with the strong
musty scent of decaying
fungi, but this year I have seen very
few fungi, and have not noticed that
odor at all,—a failure more perceptible
to frogs and toads. (Henry David Thoreau)

birth o'human nature.

Lois's house. Lake Welch. The Land.
Parkway. Calls Hollow Road. Route
202. Letchworth Village.
Stony Point. Palisades Interstate
Park. 210. Minisceonga
waterfalls.
Craterellus cantherellus.
Strawberries. *Clitopilus*
abortivus. Ramapo
Mountains. Balancing
Rock (Mother's and Dad's ashes:
where I wish mine to be scattered).
Morels formerly. *Lepiota*
procera. Cibarius. Edulis. Agaricus
campestris. Morels. Reservoir. (Map
showing locations)

Amateur.
(*The Mycophile*)

We'd said goodnight.
We drove a block east, made a U-turn.
Jap'd meanwhile
crossed the street to the
playground. He was shaking the branch

of a Ginkgo tree. Hiroshi watched
him 'till he was out of
sight.

I see a few fishes dart in the brooks.
Between winter and summer, . . . an immeasurable
interval.
(Henry David Thoreau)

Mind is not mind (in the
ordinary sense), yet it is not no-mind.
(Hsi Yun recorded by
P'ei Hsiu)

Kanawaukee Circle. Route 210. To
Southfields. To Land. (Map showing
locations and directions)

Technique (purposeless) is a
utility: it serves flexibility,
introduces the
stranger. It is not
emotionally driven: we can
safely follow it. It is inspired: it ignores
boundaries. It does not prefer
one person to another. "All Watched over by
Machines of Loving Grace."

leaves.

Giorgio, John, Lois,
John and Edith: at dawn, strawberries.

most people heAring that you know your
Mushrooms
Ask whether you've
had aNy
vIsions.
jusT
yesterdAy i received a postcard

froM people i've never met.
they had foUnd
lotS of amanitas and wanted
to know how to "deCoct from them their powers."
Am unable to help them.
some authoRs
mentIon combining the mushroom with
blueberry juice.
none, As far as i know, gives process
or quantities.

Morels
theY
Consist
enlargEd
caLled
dependIng
roUnd
froM.

Some of my friends have little interest in
mushrooms. David and M.C. used
to refuse them.
Carolyn Brown has no overwhelming desire
for them.

Deliquefy *Coprini*.

and struggle of the
Cultural Revolution.
Today, the elitist concept is dead.
Education in China is no longer
competitive and is no longer a road to
personal advancement and
status. Work in factories or in the
fields has become an accepted
part of every
child's educational experience.
(Felix Greene)

Sono
   Parecchi
hannO
  peR
conoscEre
  noStri.

Kama's on the move:
it goes as well to *Artha*
(Fuller, China) as to *Dharma.* Had
it not moved, we could have stayed with
expertise (Boulez, for example).
Just by touching, love takes place. But
now that touch must be true and
utilitarian. (*Moksha* then.) After he made
it, Fuller noticed his dome was beautiful.

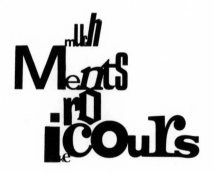

25 MESOSTICS RE AND NOT RE MARK TOBEY

it was iMpossible
    to do Anything:
the dooR
was locKed.

i won The first game.
  he wOn the second.
    in Boston,
      nExt
        Year, he'll be teaching philosophy.

                the house is a Mess:
                        pAintings
                  wheRever
                you looK.

            she told Me
              his wAy
                of Reading
    assumes that the booK he's reading is true.

why doesn'T
he stOp painting?
someBody
will havE
to spend Years cataloguing, etc.

The girl checking in the baggage
reduced Our overweight to zero
By counting it
on a first-class passEnger's ticket: the heaviest handbag
had been hidden unnecessarilY.

forTunately, we were with hanna,
antOinette,
and hanna's two Boys.
thE girl at the counter
gave one of the boYs a carry-on luggage tag as a souvenir.

My
strAtegy:
act as though you'Re home;
don't asK any questions.

instead of Music:
thunder, trAffic,
biRds, and high-speed military planes/producing sonic booms;
now and then a chicKen (pontpoint).

each Thing he saw
he asked us tO look at.
By
thE time we reached the japanese restaurant
our eYes were open.

the rooM
dAvid has in the attic
is veRy
good for his worK.

how much do The paintings
cOst?
they were Bought
on the installmEnt plan:
there was no moneY.

he played dominoes and drank calvados unTil
fOur in the morning.
carpenters came aBout
sEven
thirtY to finish their work in his bedroom.

you can find ouT
what kind Of art is up to the minute
By visiting
thE head office
of a successful advertising companY.

b a c k,

to r c a l l e s

i n h a u c e d

O e n

p h y l a b e

c o n r e e s t

c h O n g e d

t h i s

p a r t m e n t

i'M helpless:
i cAn't do a thing
without Ritty in paris
and mimi in new yorK (artservices).

"is There
anything yOu want
Brought
from thE
citY?" no, nothing. less mass media, perhaps.

waiting for the bus, i happened to look at the paveMent
i wAs standing on;
noticed no diffeRence between
looKing at art or away from it.

the chinese children accepted the freedoMs
i gAve them
afteR
my bacK was turned.

pauline served lunch on The
flOor
But
objEcted
to the waY galka was using her knife and fork.

norTh
Of paris, june '72:
collyBia platyphylla,
plutEus cervinus, pholiota
mutabilis and several *hYpholomas.*

The
dOors and windows are open.
"why Bring it back?
i'd forgottEn where it was.
You could have kept it."

he told Me
of A movie they'd seen,
a natuRe film.
he thought we would liKe it too.

The paintings
i had decided tO
Buy
wEre superfluous; nevertheless,
after several Years, i owned them.

sold Them
tO write music. now there's a third.
i must get the first two Back.
whEre
are theY?

all it is is a Melody
of mAny
coloRs:
Klangfarbenmelodie.

DIARY: HOW TO IMPROVE THE WORLD
(YOU WILL ONLY MAKE MATTERS WORSE)
CONTINUED 1971–72

CLXXIX.   Edwin Schlossberg: "Raising
animals so people will have daily
protein intake doesn't make sense; think of
all the land that's necessary for pasture."
Solution of world food problem will
involve sources of protein that stay
in position, terrarium-like places,
Fuller domes, self-supporting,
weather-controlled environments:
organic reproduction of plant foods.
Education and Ecstasy (George
Leonard).   It would be better to have no
school at all than the schools we now
have.   Encouraged, instead of
frightened, children could learn
several languages before reaching age
of four, at that age engaging in the
invention of their own languages.
Play'd be play instead of being, as now,
release of repressed anger.   **CLXXX.**
On the plane I sat next to a
psychologist employed at the
Galesburg mental hospital.   I said I was
glad students had succeeded in changing
the institution.   He said, "What are
you talking about?"   I said, I
understand patients leave the hospital
and enter enliveningly into community
life.   He said, "That isn't true."
Use the same opening until you know all its
pitfalls.   Walking toward Greenwich
and Bank Streets, I noticed an open

manhole with temporary toolshed.
Con Edison was at work.   Two tall,
    heavyset workmen, facing one another
    in the shed, were concentrating on
    something placed between them.   It
    looked as though they were playing
       chess.   I walked past, stopped, went
back, came close to them.   They *were*
    playing chess.   *CLXXXI.*   *She'd spent*
two weeks in southwest Colorado working
on Soleri's building that'll house
    three thousand people.   *All*
apartments are cubes and identical.
    Those that're finished are used by
the workers.   *"If you think about it,"*
she said, "it's awful, but if you live
in it you find it's delightful."
    Mushrooms.   Teaching-machines.
Therapy-machines aiding people to form
their brain waves, shifting waves' shape
    from that of anxiety to that of poise,
invention.   He said he'd rather have half a
    pint of the wild ones than a gallon
    of the tame (speaking of wild
strawberries).   Sam Moon, poet, met me at
the Galesburg airport.   Asked him whether
he'd heard of changes in the mental
    hospital brought about by students.
He hadn't.   Doris Moon told me hospital
    uses dope.   Doped up madmen,
formerly given jobs as salesmen, seemed
listless, not really interested in what
they were doing.   Their eyes were strange.
    Galesburg customers demanded doctors
    stop letting their patients out.
    CLXXXII.   **"Soil is as precious as**
    pearls and water as precious as oil."

(A slogan coined by the Valley of
Stones Brigade of Yueh Kechuang Commune.)
In 1959 we developed the program of
"splitting the mountain, creating the soil"
so as to alter its face into fertile land.
Doesn't matter whether you're in first
class or coach. *You see the same*
movie. **Many people are allergic to**
the commercial mushroom. **Donald M. Simons**
tells of an acquaintance who suffers
vomiting, diarrhoea and loss of
consciousness from eating any restaurant
sauce that has even a trace of a
mushroom in it. Moved to the country
for city reasons: to start summer
theatre; to set up electronic music
studio. Instead took to walking in
the woods. CLXXXIII. Just after ten
o'clock I cashed a check for one hundred
dollars. At noon I lost my billfold. I
spent the afternoon cancelling credit
cards. I also called the police. I tried
to remember what there was in my wallet
besides passport, bankbook, vaccination
certificate, and social security card. At
five o'clock I began drinking. (I was
invited to speak to staff-members of a
Connecticut asylum. After leaving the
reception room, I walked down the hall
among the madmen toward the room where I
was to speak. When I got there I knew
what had to be said. "You're sitting," I
told the doctors, "on top of a gold
mine: share your wealth with the
rest of us!") CLXXXIV. Left college
end of sophomore year. Refused honorary
degrees. Reinforcement, positive or
negative, is beside the point. I'd been

smoking like a furnace for nearly a
week.   As I was leaving, university
secretary said, "You've given us a
breath of fresh air."   *Mao: Our point of*
departure is to serve the people
whole-heartedly, to proceed in all cases
from the interests of the people and not
from one's self-interest or from the
interests of a small group.   Subjected
university library to chance
operations.   Eighty students read four
hundred books.   Class became people.
Conversation.   At nine o'clock in the
evening, the phone rang.   Man's
voice: "Did you lose anything today?"   I
lost my billfold!   "How much did you
have in it?"   Aroun' $100.   "Exactly
$98."   Where can we meet?   "Tomorrow
morning at ten-fifteen at your bank."
Which bank?   "You know which bank.   If
someone there can identify you, I'll
give you back your billfold."   I went
to sleep.   *CLXXXV.   Use what you have (no*
garbage).   Beet tops with yogurt.
Galesburg.   People still applauding our
performance.   Man, beside himself
with anger, rushed up.   Shouting, he
accused our company of fraud, me of
dishonoring Schoenberg's name.   I spoke.
He became more furious.   I was silent
but disturbed.   Madness I'd hoped for I
didn't know how to enjoy.   Future made
clear.   *I got to the bank early.   The*
manager said he'd identify me.   Sam
Moon gave me student proposal for changes
in Galesburg hospital.   He said, "It's
not what you have in mind; it's a

Skinnerian nightmare." (Teen-ager imagines
that by spending time in a building
marked Music he'll become a musician.
Even books on the subject are apt to
be confusing. I didn't learn anything to
speak of about mushrooms until I met
Guy Nearing.) CLXXXVI. (Mao: Everyone
knows that, in doing a thing, if one
does not understand its circumstances, its
characteristics and its relations to
other things, then one cannot know how
to do it, and cannot do it well.) If I
can't take what happens, I'm not
ready for anything.
Deinstitutionalization. *Opium dens in
China no longer exist. How did Chinese
shake the habit?* **Marcel Duchamp gave me a
copy of his book on King and Pawn endings.
I asked him to write something in it.
He wrote in French: Dear John look out:
yet another poisonous mushroom Marcel**
Horicon Marsh, Wisconsin, October
Seventy-one. One hundred thousand
Canadian geese. Highway 49 bisects
marsh's northern section. Bird watchers
park along the road, get out and use
binoculars. Traffic including trucks
continues, but geese seem undisturbed.
Helicopter passing over alarmed them.
As they flew up from pools and
fields, sky turned black. Traffic and
helicopter were no longer to be heard:
Goose sounds. *CLXXXVII. Edwin
Schlossberg: Gather information without
bias. Define problems. Include their
ramifications. Find solutions using
energy sources going with nature,*

not against nature (sun, wind, tides, not
        fossil fuels).   *Initiate action alone*
and with others without waiting to be told
what to do.   I waited.   10:15; 10:30;
        10:45.   I asked the bank manager
whether the branch office's address
was on my bankbook.   He assured me that
it was.   Revolution in China implemented
        in part by Big Character Posters.
People, walking in the streets,
receive instructions.   In industrialized
        West, people sit at home glued to the
        TV, or drive around listening to car
radios.   Instead of commercials,
        broadcast suggestions for useful
activity on the part of every man, woman,
and child.   Repeat every fifteen
minutes.   CLXXXVIII.   Schlossberg: Fear
        produces non-comprehensive design
science.   Commoner's proposal to send
        sewage to the land via pipeline system
        is an example.   What's needed are
        toilets automatically productive of
properly treated and packaged dry
        fertilizers.   Motel included miserable
        Chinese restaurant.   Restaurant had a
        liquor license.   Down the road was The
        Villa.   Its wine was undrinkable.
Seventeen inches of snow fell.   Winds
rose.   Traffic outlawed (state of
        emergency).   Villa closed.   Only
        restaurant open was Chinese
        restaurant.   Met in the bar, got
        plastered.   Went to dining room; food
was delicious.   Poster in River Falls,
Wisconsin: Ralph Nader has called upon
        students to organize research groups to

m
ut
grasped—hands
present
each.
evil ine,

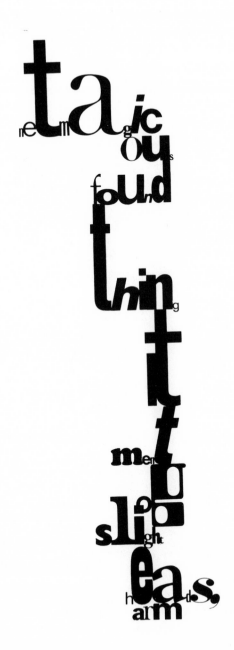

work in the public interest . . .   Corporate
Responsibility; Environmental
      Preservation; Consumer Protection; Sex
   & Race Discrimination (they must mean
Sex and Race *Liberation*); Support WISPIRG
   (Wisconsin Public Interest Research
      Group); Student Funded and
      controlled.   Sign Petition Today!
      CLXXXIX.   Ten to eleven, a slight,
elderly man entered the bank.   The
lapels of his coat were faced with fur.
We shook hands.   The bank manager said:
   It's good there're still people like you
         living.   The man replied, "I believe
      in God.   I think that doing as I do
      people prove that God exists."   Huge
747 practically empty.   Boarding pass
      lacked seat-assignment.   Hostess
dropped plan to send me back to the
counter to get one.   I'd said: There's
      plenty of room, don't you think?
We're not concerned with the audience:
      we're concerned with people.   *"In*
what does the old ideology of the
      exploiting classes lie?   It lies
essentially in self-interest—the
      natural soil for the growing of
capitalism.   That is why, in the course of
      revolution," Mao tells us, "we must
fight self."   That's why the Golden Rule
   (Do unto others as you would be done by)
   turned green in the USA.   It took
      self-interest for granted.   Devalue
it.   CXC.   Student-proposed change in
   Galesburg asylum was isolation of
patients, separation of mad from mad,

twenty-four-hour intensive supervision
of each individual. **Infirmities of old**
age. **Now that we have everything we need,**
we discover that there is almost nothing
that we have that we want. Rush hour:
no rush. Trucks, busses, cars (Sheridan
Square NYC), complete stop. Forty-five
minutes. Now and then someone moved an
inch or two. Details changed.
Congestion continued. Black truck
driver studied situation, found a
solution, cheerfully gave directions.
People clapped their hands, blew
their horns. **Early morning**
(yesterday, melting snow): sound of
footsteps; night lights still on.
CXCI. **Bank manager insisted that**
identifying me wasn't necessary: I
was one of the bank's depositors. **The**
man handed me my billfold and asked
me to look through it carefully and
notice that nothing had been removed.
First, master the endgame, then the
middle and finally the opening. Thus
you'll be able from the beginning to see
through to the end. **Mushrooms tested by**
feeding them to dog. **After dinner, maid**
said: Dog's dead. **Guests'n'hosts**
had stomachs pumped. **Dog had been run**
over by a car. *Deschool society (Ivan D.*
Illich), Education Automation (R.
Buckminster Fuller). *Just as, in*
Buddhism, denial of cause and effect
arose from the realization that
everything's caused by everything
else, so Illich's society without

school isn't different from Fuller's
society with nothing but school.
Illich and Fuller: All there is to do
is live and learn.   **CXCII.**   **"A little**
child shall lead them."   **Edwin**
Schlossberg's Brooklyn Children's
Museum.   **Eddie insisted Board of**
Directors include children.   **When**
Schlossberg visited Fuller, Bucky said,
"Listen carefully to the children's
words.   **I want to know each word they**
say."   *County in Florida.*   *Law was*
passed prohibiting the sale of
detergents.   *Housewives travelled to*
other counties to purchase their
detergents.   *"We know we're breaking*
the law but we want to get our clothes
white."   **While looking through my**
billfold I said, I want to share what's
in it with you: $50.   **He didn't smile.**
"My work's time-consuming.   **This has**
been a serious interruption."   **I gave**
him another $20.   **What do you do?**   **"I'm**
in Rewrite."   **What's that?**   **"It's in**
connection with Continuity."   **What's your**
name?   **"So-and-So."**   CXCIII.   Valda
said that if you change your residence
every six months you can legally free
your children from compulsory
education.   I asked Mr. So-and-So
whether he had found my billfold in a taxi.
He said, "I found it in the gutter."
How old are you, dear moon?
Thirteen-seven?   **You're still young, are**
you not?   **One comes, then another, and**
another.   **Who'll be held on your lap?**
America's the oldest country of the

twentieth century.   It's made the most
mistakes of the twentieth century.   **Whole
Earth.**   Industrialization is a
self-regenerative evolutionary phenomenon
which started in China at least four
thousand years ago.   It travelled
westward, and has reached China again
in vastly advanced effectiveness.
(R. Buckminster Fuller.)   CXCIV.   Ihab
Hassan's book, *The Dismemberment of
Orpheus,* begins with a statement by
Franz Kafka: "The decisive moment in
human evolution is perpetual.   That is
why the revolutionary spiritual
movements that declare all former things
worthless are in the right, for
nothing has yet happened."   ***Whole
Earth Cook Book.***   **Our recipes are not
complicated: we want to turn you on to
the relaxation in simple, natural
cooking.   The country kitchen is a
traditional gathering place.   We at
the Whole Earth Restaurant make a
party out of preparing meals.   We hope
you'll do the same.   (Cadwallader and
Ohr.)**   *Mao: Destruction means criticism
and repudiation; it means revolution.
It involves reasoning things out, which
is construction.   Put destruction
first, and in the process you have
construction.*   CXCV.   I complimented Mr.
So-and-So on the tie he was wearing.
It was silk, dark red, straight and
narrow; it was pinned against a pink and
white striped shirt.   He said, "It's a
relic of a previous age."   *As we
left the bank, there was Meg Harper, one*

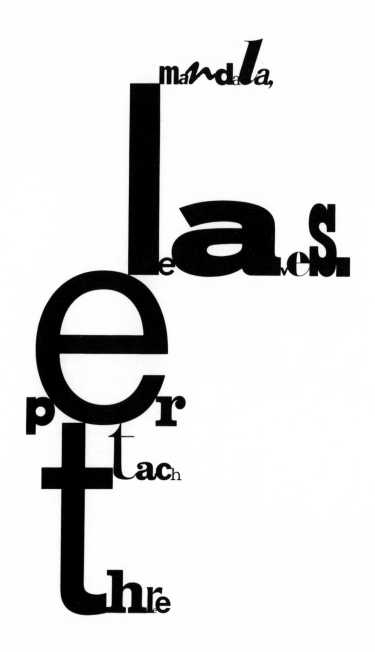

of the Cunningham dancers.   *I introduced
her to Mr. So-and-So and told him that
the Cunningham Company was about to
open in Brooklyn.*   *I offered to
arrange for him to have tickets.*   *Mr.
So-and-So said, "Thank you, but I
don't want any reward."*   All night
long, thoughts of nirvana and samsara.
How exhausting!   Apparently I was caught
by the Buddha.   (Sengai.)   CXCVI.
Mushrooms I found in one day were more
than enough for a year.   **Reduce use of
combustion engines.**   **Jim'n'Carolyn went
to skyscraper Indian restaurant.
Restaurant had no other customers.
Food'n'view were good.**   **Afterwards,
back home, Jim noticed he didn't have
his wallet.**   **Suzuki Daisetz: One has
not understood Zen until one has forgotten
it.**   We got rid of the wolves.   Now there
are too many deer.   Forest ranger's
proposal to reintroduce wolves was
stymied by protests from
profit-seeking sheepranchers.   The
shepherd is a wolf in man's clothing.   I
haven't been to a movie for three
months of Sundays.   I gather from what
Carolyn reports that Hollywood now
produces false entertainment: unmitigated
violence on the screen; snickering,
laughter in the audience.   CXCVII.   Jim
telephoned the restaurant: Do you have my
wallet?   "Yes.   Do you have our
seat-cover?"   I don't know anything
about your seat-cover.   I just want my
wallet back.   "We've lost too many
seat-covers and recently, also, a vase; if

you'll bring us back our seat-cover we'll
gladly return your wallet."   Thruways
promote the automobile industry.
People without high-speed cars can't
use them.   They're "false utility"
(Illich).   Variation: multiplying cans and
bottles provides false convenience.
Let each household keep its containers,
taking them empty to appropriate stores
to be filled.   This'll bring about
refreshing changes in supermarket
design.   Staying at home'll become
as amusing as vacationing in a village
in Spain.   **CXCVIII.**   **Needed new glasses.**
Doctor, noticing hemorrhages in my eyes,
said, "Do you have diabetes?"   Don'know.
Disturbed, looked up diabetes in
dictionary, decided I wasn't overly hungry,
thirsty, didn't excessively urinate.
Complete examination showed no
diabetes.   Eye-doctor said, "Well,
you're just getting old.   There's nothing
I can do about it.   I want to see you
every two or three months."   Bantam
paperback anthology of the writings of Mao
Tse-tung, edited by Ann Freemantle, is
dedicated to Dr. Ivan D. Illich.   Twelve
disciples.   One teacher.   One too
many.   Best things in life're free;
American industry thinks we can't afford
them.   If we could change our language,
that's to say the way we think,
we'd probably be able to swing the
revolution.   *CXCIX.   On his way to*
the restaurant Jim decided that if
they refused to give him his wallet he'd
get a policeman to help him.   **We must**

find something else to do than art:
we are going to China.   We hope our visit
will leave no traces.   Called Statistics
Section, Immigration Division, Canadian
Government, asked how many Americans
had recently become Canadian
citizens.   They said: That takes five
years.   However, in 1967, 19,038
Americans immigrated to Canada.   In
1968, 20,422.   In 1969, 22,785.   In 1970,
24,424.   USA has apparently taken
steps to solve the population
problem, but only from its own point
of view.   CC.   Jack Collins, brilliant
mind, spastic paraplegic, Bobby
Fischer's teacher.   No one in the world of
chess is as beloved.   Frequently
laughing, he gets around the apartment by
riding small tricycle.   People who
don't play complain chess takes too much
time.   Given the opportunity to study with
Collins, it'd be a waste of time not
to.   Cherish and reuse plastic utensils and
containers.   Don't throw'em away;
don't acquire more than you need.   Don't
take'em with you; leave them for the next
person to use.   Distinguish, as you
would in the case of mushrooms, between
those that're poisonous and those
that aren't.   Do not use plastics that are
derived from fossil fuels.   CCI.   Midst of
these thoughts, Jim felt unusual
warmth on his back.   Reaching under his
coat, he found the seat-cover stuck
to his jacket.   Receiving his
wallet, his apologies were politely
interrupted.   "Don't apologize: this

happens all the time." **Alternatives to**
art. Crossing bridge from Windsor, Canada,
to Detroit, Michigan, the bus driver
announced: We're now entering No Man's
Land. **A newspaperman wrote asking me to**
send'im my philosophy in a nutshell.
Get out of whatever cage you happen to
be in. If you're a dope addict in Detroit
and happen to be hospitalized for some
reason, no problem. Someone pays you a
visit, brings you a fix, and, on the
way out, rips what he can from other
patients. ⸴CCII. Irritation in my left
eye was diagnosed by two doctors as
chalazion. "Is that a sty?" No, it's
chalazion. "Will it go away by itself?"
No, it has to be scraped out. *Sue Weil*
made an appointment for me in
Minneapolis four days thence which I
kept even though my eye no longer
bothered me. The doctor's office was a
museum of modern art, plus many
patients and many nurses. One cheerful
nurse gave me a preliminary
examination. National Wildlife
Refuges: museumization of
wilderness. Controlled folly. **Doctor**
said, "Your eyes're healthy.
Nothing needs to be done." What about the
hemorrhages? "They're not significant.
The sty will go away in six or eight
months." What about the chalazion?
"Chalazion's a synonym for sty." *CCIII.*
Choose among all the masters the master
whose way of playing appeals to you
the most. Then replay all of his
games. **Barbershop's like a community.**

Once you get in you don't want to leave.
It's for men, women, and children.
There are potted plants, flowers, two
large live tortoises.   Brightly
colored robes to choose from.
Antenna Enterprises.   Cry in the
wilderness.   We're indebted to China for
its language, the I Ching, Lao-tse,
Chuang-tse, Zen Buddhism too.   Gunpowder
we'll do without; printing'll be
electronic.   The Great Wall and roast
pig, together with other meats, can go.
Give us the Chinese sense of nature,
the Chinese sense of society.   *CCIV.*
As we were taking off from Detroit,
asked the Chinaman sitting near me
whether he thought acupuncture might be
used to de-addict drug addicts.   He
said, "Works for arthritis and lung
diseases."   You think it works for drug
addiction?   "Perhaps it does," he said.
Imitation of nature in her manner of
operation, traditionally the artist's
function, is now what everyone has
to do.   Complicate your garden so it's
surprising like uncultivated land.
Suburban policeman came to the door; he
went away without making any arrests.
If you're poor, its illegal.   If you're
rich, you're automatically within the
law.   *What necessary mystery can*
many people working together make?
Effective revolution.   Norman Brown:
What we finally seek to do is to create
an environment that works so well we
can run wild in it.   CCV.   Fuller: I now
ask cosmic questions.   "Is man needed

in the universe?"   "Does he have a
universal function?"   "If he is essential
what needs to be invented to improve his
    functioning?"   "What are the largest
overall trends of human evolution that
need accommodations?"   Food.   *Infirmities
of old age (old Japanese sayings):*
    wrinkles on the face, dark spots grow
    on the skin, and the back bent,
    bald-headed and grey-bearded, the
hands tremble, the legs totter, and gone
    are the teeth, hard of hearing and
        eyesight bedimmed, indispensable are
    a hood on the head, wrappers, a stick,
    and spectacles,   **Syntax, like**
government, can only be obeyed.   It is
        therefore of no use except when you
        have something particular to command
        such as: Go buy me a bunch of carrots.
The mechanism of the I Ching, on the other
        hand, is a utility.   Applied to
        letters and aggregates of letters, it
        brings about a language that can be
enjoyed without being understood.   CCVI.
then a hot-water bottle, heating stone,
        chamber pot, and a back-scratcher;
meddlesome he is, afraid of dying, and
        lonesome; suspicious of others, the
desire for possession grows stronger;
repetitive, short-tempered and querulous;
obtrusive and officious; the same
stories over and over again in which his
        own children are invariably praised;
boastful of his health, he makes others
        feel tired beyond endurance.   "It is
        right to rebel."   When I had a Jaguar, I
    noticed anyone else who drove a

Jaguar.   Now I'm wearing jeans instead of
suits, I notice nearly everyone.   **Fuller**
and Mao.   Transform mistakes into
    projects, misinformation into facts.
Forget yourself.   Blur the distinction
    between Fuller and Mao.   Change the
    environment and at the same time
change man.   There is no line to be
    drawn between the two.   CCVII.
Gautham told me Indian weavers used to
    work alone.   To increase production,
assembly line methods introduced at
    Ahmedabad.   Workmen became unhappy.
    After systematic experiments, group
    cooperation without unhappiness was
    established.   Five people make smallest
    happy group.   Less than five make
trouble for one another.   Twelve make
largest happy group; with thirteen group
    spirit is lost.   We have learned that
    from here on it is success for all or
    for none.   "Unity is plural and at
    minimum two."   You and I are inherently
different and complementary.   Together we
average as zero, that is, as eternity.
    (Buckminster Fuller.)   **Two: one against**
one.   CCVIII.   Mao Tse-tung: We must firmly
believe that the great majority of the
    masses are good and that bad elements
only make up a very small fraction.   **Three**
people are two against the other one.
    Four people split into two couples, each
    couple intent on making trouble for
the other couple.   Old age of the USA.   It
can't see or hear very well.   It's hard
    for it to walk.   Its face is
    wrinkled; its teeth're false.   *Black*

mother'n'son in the laundromat.   She
was born in Barbados, went to Europe,
married a doctor, became a trained
nurse.   Boy was born in Toronto.
Jobs she takes are those permitting her
son to accompany her.   When washing machine
I was using began dancing, she helped
me hold it in place.

Title design for *M* by Raymond M. Grimaila

The text was composed by the Eastern Typesetting Company. The type faces used are Weiss Roman, Times Roman, Times Roman Bold, Memphis Medium, Baskerville, Spartan Medium, Spartan Heavy, Garamond, Bodoni Bold, and Century Schoolbook.

Mureau was typewritten by the author using an I.B.M. Selectric II with seventeen elements.

This book was printed by the Halliday Lithograph Corporation and bound by Stanhope Bindery.

Designed with the aid of I Ching chance operations

Wesleyan University Press, *Middletown, Connecticut*